TALES OF WONDER

ALSO BY HUSTON SMITH

Is There a Universal Grammar of Religion?
(with Henry Rosemont, Jr.)

A Seat at the Table: Struggling for American Indian Religious Freedom (with Phil Cousineau)

The Soul of Christianity: Restoring the Great Tradition

Conversations with Huston Smith on the Spiritual Life
(with Phil Cousineau)

Buddhism: A Concise Introduction (with Philip Novak)

Islam: A Concise Introduction

Why Religion Matters: The Fate of the Human Spirit in an Age of Disbelief

Cleansing the Doors of Perception: The Religious Significance of Entheogenic Plants and Chemicals

One Nation Under God: The Triumph of the Native American Church (edited with Reuben Snake)

Forgotten Truth: The Common Vision of the World's Religions

Huston Smith: Essays on World Religion
(edited by M. Darrol Bryant)

The World's Religions: Our Great Wisdom Traditions

Beyond the Postmodern Mind: The Place of Meaning in a Global Civilization

The Purposes of Higher Education

To Lyn
love, Jen

Christmas 2010

Tales of Wonder

Adventures Chasing the Divine

AN AUTOBIOGRAPHY

HUSTON SMITH

WITH

JEFFERY PAINE

HarperOne
An Imprint of HarperCollinsPublishers

HarperOne

HarperCollins books may be purchased for educational, business, or sales promotional use. For information please write: Special Markets Department, HarperCollins Publishers, 10 East 53rd Street, New York, NY 10022.

HarperCollins Web site: http://www.harpercollins.com

HarperCollins®, ♛®, and HarperOne™ are trademarks of HarperCollins Publishers

FIRST EDITION

Library of Congress Cataloging-in-Publication Data is available.

Smith, Huston.
Tales of wonder : adventures chasing the divine : an autobiography / Huston Smith and Jeffery Paine.—1st ed.
    p. cm.
ISBN 978-0-06-115426-3

1. Smith, Huston. 2. Religious biography. I. Paine, Jeffery. II. Title.
BL73.S645A3 2009
200.92—dc22
[B]   2008055099

09 10 11 12 13 RRD (H) 10 9 8 7 6 5 4 3 2 1

To Kendra

"I asked so much of you
in this brief lifetime,
Perhaps we'll meet again
in the childhood of the next."

from a love poem by the Sixth Dalai Lama

Tell me a story.
In this century, and moment, of mania,
Tell me a story.
Make it a story of great distances, and starlight.
The name of the story will be Time,
But you must not pronounce its name.
Tell me a story of deep delight.

Robert Penn Warren

Look at this, you scornful souls, and lose yourselves in
    wonder.
For in your day I do such deeds that, if men were to
    tell you this
Story, you would not believe it.

St. Paul (speaking for God), Acts 12

Wonderful the Presence
One sees in the present.
Oh wonder-struck am I to see
Wonder on wonder.

the Adi Granth *(the sacred book of Sikhism)*

CONTENTS

FOREWORD

No Wasted Journeys

"BE NOT SIMPLY *GOOD*—BE GOOD FOR SOMETHING," HENRY David Thoreau wrote with typical force to a new friend, Harrison Blake, who had just approached him by letter. "To set about living a true life," he had declared a few paragraphs earlier, "is to go [on] a journey to a distant country, gradually to find ourselves surrounded by new scenes and men." Thoreau's injunction was as much to the point as it was characteristic. Many people can share a certain light with us, the fruits of their explorations, and in that very transmission there is a special beauty and value; but the ones who really move us are sharing with us their lives, showing us how the principles they elucidate play out in the here and now. Aldous Huxley, lifelong experimenter, did not just write on the religions of the world; he tried, as far as possible, to live them. The Fourteenth Dalai Lama has not been merely a monk sitting in a remote kingdom, offering a model of clarity and goodness to his people; he has brought the values and ideas for which he speaks right into the heart of hard-core Realpolitik in Washington and Beijing, into the urgency of trying to protect six million people under occupation, into the center of our mixed-up modern media circus.

Long before I had ever met Huston Smith, I felt drawn to
this celebrated explorer of the great traditions because of my
sense that he was not just teaching but living and acting. I
went to hear him onstage and noticed how the lucidity and
purity for which he spoke were also *how* he spoke; this was
no mere scholar telling us what he read, but someone passing on, with an infectious sweetness and integrity, what he
had learned traveling to India, putting himself through the
rigors of Zen practice in Japan, hitchhiking across the American West to listen to Gerald Heard, becoming the one to record Tibetan multiphonic chanting in the Himalayas. When
I saw him speaking to Bill Moyers in a classic series of public-television interviews about the exploration of the Real and
universal understanding, I realized these were far more than
words; here was the rare professor who does yogic headstands,
observes the Islamic rule, regularly reads scriptures from the
eight major traditions—and goes to his local church (as well,
of course, as seeing that even television can be a mass means to
the useful end of disseminating ideas). A little later I was not
surprised to learn that he had been a good friend of the Fourteenth Dalai Lama for more than forty years—acknowledged
twice as a teacher by the Dalai Lama in his 2005 book on science; had been the one to introduce Aldous Huxley properly
to Alan Watts; had, in fact, been not just a beloved professor for half a century, who did as much as anyone to bring
the world into the minds of Americans, but also a tireless explorer who really did meet Eleanor Roosevelt and Martin
Luther King and witnessed the founding of the United Nations and the uprising at Tiananmen Square.

The first time I met him, I asked him if he had ever met
Thomas Merton, and he told me the beautiful story, herein

alluded to, of how he found himself in Calcutta in 1968 and went out into a garden where a man was sitting with a soft drink, as if waiting for him. It just happened to be the man he most wanted to meet in all the world (and who would be dead, tragically, within a few weeks). Some would call this characteristic luck; to me it sounded like a kind of grace.

Professor Smith has irreversibly changed and lightened and broadened the lives of millions of students and believers (and, no less important, nonbelievers) through his classic books, and those books have changed as the times have changed. He's best remembered, no doubt, for the essential introduction to the world's great traditions, *The World's Religions,* from 1964, which brought Buddhism, Hinduism, and Islam into many American lives and households long before *karma* and *nirvana* were common terms; what distinguishes that work, even today, is how it sits inside every tradition that it describes, blending the rigorous eye of the scholarly outsider with the beating heart of the initiate. Like a kind of Method scholar, the author seems to report on each tradition from the inside out, as it might seem to one of its adherents, and in the process what he manages to do, without tendentiousness or strain, is to light up the places where religions converge without ever denying the ineffaceable differences between them (and the danger of following a "salad bar" technique in which, by combining the elements of many faiths, one loses the depth of all).

In later times, though, he has pushed this exploratory spirit further and deeper, defending religion against the reductions of "scientism" (a task for which his fifteen years teaching at MIT well prepared him), fashioning, as Carl Gustav Jung might have done, a universal grammar of religion, even detailing, in later books (as very few learned religious scholars might) what he has learned from Native American traditions and even from psychoactive plants and chemicals. (In his seventies he was traveling down to Mexico to participate in all-night vigils of the indigenous people, whose beliefs he felt he had not done justice to before.) Though the field of comparative religions is sometimes said to have begun with William James, Professor Smith has in his way created his own field, by not really comparing religions so much as encountering each one in turn and trying to find its burning core as well as its philosophical uniqueness. And when, in recent years, religion came under new attack, both from postmodern skepticism and from regular people appalled by what is being done in its name, he came forth with a closely argued defense of the best side of religion (finding best sides has always been his gift), *Why Religion Matters,* nine months before the attacks of September 11 made such a defense imperative.

Yet for all this learning and philosophical tenacity, I don't think Huston Smith would have the authority and the humanity that are so luminous in him had he just been sitting in a library, absorbing texts. A few years ago, at the *Los Angeles Times* Festival of Books, where more than 350 authors appear every spring, I found myself simply beaming as I listened to him conduct an onstage conversation; the reason, though I could barely say it to myself, was that his presence and the way he spoke both embodied and infectiously passed on the life of intelligence and adventure. Here was someone who could remind us that *integrity* means wholeness, and who could point out that religion needs science as much as science needs religion, since neither can give us the entire picture. Here, too, was someone who had worked hard to ease the passageway and brighten the conversation between theory and praxis. "Let nothing," as Thoreau wrote in his letter, "come between you and the light."

This distinction—between those who expound religion and those who experience it, between those who talk about spiritual radiance and those who cast it—has always been close to the center of many of our most potent conundrums: how can that wise man act in so seemingly foolish or ungenerous a way; and how is it, conversely, that that person of almost tangible goodness cannot give us the words for what she is feeling and doing? The first by-product of thinking about spiritual truth, often, is the creation of a palace that one cannot muster the discipline to live in. Professor Smith, for me and I think for thousands of others who have been transformed by him, has not only inhaled the wisdom—and, he always stresses, a sense of the limits—of the great traditions, but also lived with suffering, long enough, perhaps, to see that easy solutions and grand theories will not do.

Small wonder that he has been everywhere, in our public and private life, for more than six decades now; or that his autobiography—as, indeed, with such friends of his as Merton, Huxley, and the Dalai Lama—has the outlines of a spiritual classic, of a soul's lifelong dance with what is real. Jung, for example, worked as hard as anyone in the twentieth century to elucidate the workings of the mind; but the book of his that speaks to many a reader today, even in high school classes, is his autobiography, *Memories, Dreams, Reflections,* which he wrote almost in spite of himself and reluctantly in his eighties.

In his later years, Professor Smith has been bringing this personal dimension to more and more of his scholarly writings, in his 2005 book, *The Soul of Christianity,* lighting up the tradition in which he was born and raised as if walking through a series of chapels, excitedly, with a candle. There are no conditions placed upon his dissemination of the truth, and you feel how what he cares about has played out in his pulse and in his heart.

I will not detain the reader any longer when she has almost nine decades of grand and illuminating adventures to devour; all I will say is that the last time I saw Professor Smith, at Grace Cathedral in San Francisco, when he was eighty-six and being feted by many of his grateful admirers, he came into the great chapel looking a little frail, first in a wheelchair and then being supported by his wife of sixty-four years, Kendra, a daughter, and a grandson. He proceeded to address his friends in fluent Chinese, to go up to the podium and speak movingly of his parents, and then—after Sufi dancers and Ch'an priests and Buddhist scholars had shared their thoughts with him—to dance down the aisle of the cathedral to the sound of pounding drums.

As I watched him move out toward the daylight, leaving his wheelchair behind and more full of life and excitement at eighty-six than I had been in my thirties, I recalled that it had been his example, his life, and the singular fortune—though I would call it grace—of his life's pilgrimage that we would remember as much as we did his wisdom, his brilliance, and his breadth. "I do believe," Thoreau told his friend in 1848, "that the outward and the inward life correspond."

Pico Iyer
New Camaldoli,
Big Sur, California
March 2009

PROLOGUE

The Explorer

A HINDU TEACHER OF MINE WARNED ME YEARS AGO THAT if I did not write my life story I would be reborn pen in hand. So with pen—or rather, computer—in hand now, I begin of all my books the one strangest and closest to me. I step from behind the curtains—from behind my previous books and subjects: comparative religion, primordial wisdom, postmodernity, science versus scientism—to meet you, as it were, face-to-face.

From a lifetime of a million moments, how does one select the one to begin such a tale? I will choose three moments, seemingly inconsequential, to introduce you to the boy, the young man, and now the old man you will meet in these pages.

The child. From my earliest memories: whenever my family went anywhere I would bring back a stone to put in our yard. Even as a small boy I felt that every encounter, each experience—even a symbol or token of it—was to be kept and cherished.

The young man. In college one of my jobs was opening the school cafeteria at 6:30 a.m. However, I didn't own an

A spiritual teacher told me that if I did not write my autobiography, I would be reborn "pen in hand." He did not say anything about my dying pen in hand. That may happen, too.

alarm clock. Another student left the boarding house at six, so I asked him to wake me. Recently he reminded me that I awoke the same way every morning. I would shoot bolt upright in bed, stretch out my arms, and yell, "Good!" I may wake up differently today, but I still say under my breath a loud *good* to the world.

The old man. Not long ago I was in the hospital for cochlear-implant surgery that my primary physician had advised me against having. I was nearing ninety, and she was not sure I would survive hours under anesthesia. I overrode her advice: I would not be borderline deaf; I wanted to hear what my family, my friends, and the world have to say. Just when the gurney was to wheel me into the operating room, a nurse announced that the surgery had been temporarily delayed. My wife, Kendra, knew I loved to sing, so she suggested we

Portrait of the Seeker as a Young Man. When I was in college, so a college roommate recently reminded me, I awoke the same way every morning. I would shoot bolt upright in bed, stretch out my arms full length, and shout *Good! Good* is the world and all its wonders.

sing, and sing we did for the next hour. Since I've always been a voracious traveler, one song we sang was "The Wayward Wind":

> Oh the wayward wind is a restless wind,
> A restless wind that yearns to wander;
> And he was born the next of kin,
> The next of kin to the wayward wind.

There I was, facing a life-threatening operation, and we were singing and quite happy, as so often we had been in the past.

⬚ ⬚ ⬚

It might seem that I came to my career—teaching and writing about religion—by inheritance. As the child of missionaries in China, I grew up in a home saturated in religion. We began every morning with *pa zung*, prayers, in which our Chinese servants would join us. Mother led us in singing a hymn, and then Father read from the Bible in Chinese, with our cook helping him when he stumbled over the words. Then we would all kneel while father said a closing prayer. The day had now begun.

Parental influence and environment and education—they all figure in, but they cannot fully explain the turn our lives take. My brother Walt had the same upbringing, and religion bores him. Our lives are wrapped in mystery, and a lifetime is hardly sufficient to begin to fathom it. An image I find useful is the cross—not the Christian cross, but an ordinary cross. One beam of the cross is horizontal, which stands for the historical dimension: our life amid observable events and calendar time. The other beam, the vertical, thrusts upward toward heaven and suggests the sacred dimension: our lives amid timeless truths. We live in time and timelessness simultaneously, just as we are simultaneously body, mind, and spirit.

And it is as a body, a mind, and a spirit that I begin each day. First upon waking I do physical exercise for my body. I favor India's hatha yoga, a sequence of *asanas,* or postures, that culminate in the headstand. (Yoga has stood me in good

My grandson Isaiah. When my daughter Karen married Zhenya, it opened a door to Judaism for me. Throughout my life doors to the world's religions kept opening to me, in ways never anticipated.

stead. One maddeningly beautiful spring day I held my distracted students' attention by teaching the class while standing on my head.) The body thus nurtured, I turn to mind and to spirit.

For my mind I slowly read a few pages from the Bible or a bible (the Bhagavad Gita, the Tao Te Ching, the Qur'an, the Sufi poems of Rumi, and so on). Now more mentally alert, I come to the spirit. For the spirit, I pray. I pray for those I know who are in trouble of one sort or another. Having prayed for others, I now pray for myself, which involves introspection—am I happy, sad, or anxious?—so I know what to pray for. Then I empty my mind of all thoughts and dwell in the luminous consciousness that underlies thinking. I conclude by repeating three times the Jesus Prayer of Eastern Orthodoxy for mercy: "Lord Jesus Christ, Son of God, have mercy on me, a sinner."

At the end of my morning ritual, I review the upcoming day. I survey its anticipated events and deliberate how to make my responses adequate, and I pray my actions shall occur in both dimensions—the historical and the vertical—simultaneously. OK, done; time for coffee; time to begin.

Truth in advertising: I am not a religious scholar. What I do is try to show people how they can get something of value personally from religion, which is why I concentrate on its positive side. How you might label me is "religious communicator."

One day I received by mail an envelope addressed in a child's scrawl to Mr. Smith. I opened it and read, "We are studying religion. We do not know about religion. Will you tell us about religion? The Third Grade." I dialed the phone number included and arranged with the teacher to meet her class on the following Friday.

When I stepped into the classroom, a blast of energy nearly knocked me off my feet. This was last period, and the day was Friday, and the kids were wired to be out of there. Don't lecture to them, I thought. Nothing you say can possibly get through. It has to be *action.*

"You asked me to tell you about religion," I began. "Have you ever heard of Japan?" Arms waved all over the room.

"Good," I continued. "We will do religion the way they do it in Japan." I now had some of their attention.

"When the Japanese do religion they sit on the floor." Melee and glee ensued as the kids pushed their desks to the wall, intentionally bumping into other desks in the process. On the teacher's desk I assumed the full-lotus position and asked, "Can you sit that way?"

Several show-offs could, but I assured the others that sitting cross-legged was just as good. "How long can you sit this way?"

"Five minutes," one girl said.

A boy topped her: "Fifteen minutes!"

Most of the kids could sit that way only a minute, and some lasted only a few seconds before breaking into giggles. But nobody was bored now or thinking about the weekend. It made a good start, and the rest of the class was fun. Afterward several kids stopped by the desk to say good-bye, and one asked if I liked jellybeans. I said yes, especially black ones, and he sorted from his bag all the black ones and thrust them into my hand.

In 2001 my *Why Religion Matters* received the Wilbur Award for the best book on religion addressed to the general public. The only prize I value more came in the mail the week after my visit to the third-graders: a bag of black jellybeans.

░ ░ ░

All books have one, and perhaps only one, thing in common: they each have a title. Coming up with possible titles is the most playful part of writing a book. Here are some possible titles for the volume you are holding, which like pet doves I now set free.

First rejected title. The Sri Lankan polymath Ananda Coomaraswamy tells us that the best tombstone would have chiseled on it *Hic Jacket Nomo* ("Here lies no one"). Coomaraswamy's point is that life's greatest success is getting rid of your finite ego. I tend to agree, but with my clamoring ego solidly in place, I considered the title *Memories of a Failed Nobody.*

Second rejected title: No Wasted Journey. As the hemlock poison began taking effect, Socrates reported to his companions, "To my surprise my impending death holds no terror for me." Either death will be a peaceful sleep, or better yet, Socrates said, we will travel to Hades and meet "the heroes of old who lived just lives in their day. *No wasted journey,* that." When I first read it, the phrase "no wasted journey" pierced me like an arrow. I was a young man and felt I could not live without seeing every marvel the world offered. And usually when not teaching I was to be found, unpredictably, on one of the six continents (never Antarctica) on some journey, seeing some of the world's wonder.

Third rejected title. The first poem I ever committed to memory, around age fourteen, was Rudyard Kipling's "The Explorer." In it the narrator has settled down, built his barns, and strung his fences, because that's what sensible people say to do. But a bad conscience nags him night and day:

> Something hidden, go and find it;
> Go and look behind the ranges.
> Something lost behind the ranges;
> Lost and waiting for you—go!

"The Explorer" haunts me, even in my old age. My curiosity continues unabated, continues to find the world a fascination. An explorer's legs keep moving forward—the direction mine always chose to go.

The title I did choose. When finally I decided to write my memoirs, I told Kendra that I now planned to do what I had vowed never to do. Kendra said, "Good. I have the title for you." She quoted these lines from Robert Penn Warren:

> Make it a story of great distances, and starlight.
> The name of the story will be Time,
> But you must not pronounce its name.
> Tell me a story of deep delight.

An earlier line in the poem says to tell "tales of wonder." And so, it is as *Tales of Wonder* that this book—my life, dear reader—now comes into your hands.

TALES OF WONDER

PART ONE

The Horizontal Dimension

My Life in Historical Time

I

COMING OF AGE
IN A SACRED UNIVERSE

AS I WRITE THESE WORDS, MY NINETIETH BIRTHDAY LIES over the horizon. It is hardly unusual to encounter a ninety-year-old today. Nor does it feel "unusual" to be ninety. When I look out, my eyes take in what anybody would see. But once. . . . No, let us begin properly: *Once upon a time, long ago and far away,* there was a boy who saw a world no one will see the likes of again.

When I compare my childhood to a boy's or girl's today, I realize, in retrospect, that mine took place in a garden of *never-agains. Probably never again:* shall a boy grow up so isolated from the bigger world, in a place so self-contained that it made its own little world. *Probably never again:* shall a child's days be so simple. (I could not petulantly pout, "Don't want this—want that!" because there was only *this* and no *that.*) *Probably never again:* shall opposites—life and death, rich and poor—be so close as to seem two sides of the same coin. *And surely never again:* shall existence be so uncluttered by technology, so gadget- and distraction-free. Every sound I heard was natural or human-made. Ours was basic Life 101.

My early memories might be pictures in a medieval man-uscript rather than belonging to someone still living in the twenty-first century. My childhood took place in rural China, and indeed the town where my parents were missionaries had a medieval wall around it. At ten at night the town gates were locked, to keep out thieves, and the town crier beat his bamboo stick against a gong—*gwang, gwang, gwang*—to scare off robbers. Within the town wall nothing—in a way not even our body parts and body functions—resembled its counterpart today. Our *amah,* or nanny, had "golden lotuses," those bound feet so prized (by men) in old China. I recall watching, with horror and fascination, her unwrapping the horrid, smelly bandages from her feet each evening. Inside our home we had no flush toilet; rather, a "night-soil harvester" carted away our bowel movements for fertilizer, leaving us in exchange a few small coins. The town wall kept out not only thieves and robbers; it shut out almost everything you would be familiar with today, which in any case had not been invented or simply was not available there.

It was a self-contained world. In our small town, named Dzang Zok, no movies, television—much less the Internet—existed to bring the faraway near. There were no telephones whose ringing would have inserted *elsewhere* into *here.* By the time a newspaper finally reached us, its news was history. If we eventually had a sort of radio, it was because my clever older brother built his own crystal wireless set. It received a grand total of one station, broadcast from Shanghai, sixty-five miles away. When we called our *amah* in to listen to it, she circled it, wary of the demon inside the contraption. It was easier to believe that a hidden sprite was talking than that a box could.

Except for that radio, no traffic, no automobiles, no sirens, no planes overhead intruded; not even a dentist's drill

The youngest churchgoer in China.
I am standing outside my father's church in Dzang Zok. Soon I would start my own church—in our toolshed: I played minister and the neighborhood Chinese boys and girls were my parishioners.

hummed. There was little in the way of machinery or technology in the town: our coal-stoked generator provided our house with the only electricity in the area. With no other electric lights and also with no pollution in rural China then, from our backyard I gazed at the same night sky a hermit on a Himalayan mountaintop might see, infinitely star-lit and glittering.

As an adult, after living in America, I returned to China on a visit. I tentatively asked the elevator man in our Shanghai hotel if my Chinese was still understandable. When he nodded, I explained, since I spoke not in a Mandarin but a Shanghai dialect, "I am a Shanghai man."

"Noooo!" he said.

I then named the city nearer to the town where I grew up. "I am a Soochow man."

"Nooooooooo!"

He shook a finger at me. "You are Dzang Zok man!" The globe today is one interconnected overlapping network, but my accent still marked me from one tiny dot, Dzang Zok, which in my boyhood was the whole world.

[5]

The town of long ago and far away. Dzang Zok was in many ways more a town of the Middle Ages than one of today. You can just make out part of the medieval wall that encircled the town.

Within that small world there was a smaller world. We were the only Caucasian family in Dzang Zok, practically a law unto ourselves. My father was every (white) father; my mother, every mother. I knew only one way things could be. I did not wonder whether to become a fireman, baseball player, or president when I grew up; only one profession was imaginable: missionary. Going from home to school was not the shock of strangeness many six-year-olds feel; for me it meant walking to the dining-room table, where my mother taught me and my two brothers. I can remember my very first lesson. Mother described a blind man who, bumping into a tree, asked what it was. Upon being told a tree, he said, "I see." I wrote down my first words: I SEE. My mother taught with such gentleness that I never realized I was an agonizingly slow learner. Had I gone to a public school, and not received the atten-

The tower that dominated our town. All such towers have seven stories to represent the seven heavens and a roof to ward off the rain.

tion she lavished, I might have been segregated into a class for "special" children.

And opposites and contraries were neighbors there. Death was too common in Dzang Zok to be hidden away. My parents' first child, Moreland, died on his second Christmas Eve. Our male cook's son died in the night, and I remember thinking it strange to see a man weeping. An irrepressible, high-spirited missionary visited us, and the next day he ate contaminated food and died. My parents grieved for Moreland; our cook grieved for his male baby; I grieved for the fun-loving missionary. My earliest memory is of the precariousness of life—of being on fire with a raging fever, when I was rationed to one teaspoonful of boiled water every forty-five minutes, for that was all I could keep down. What's different (from now), however, is that though people suffered and grieved, they did not live in fear of the Dark Stranger. Death was not a thing apart, an "unnatural" tragedy, nor for the religious was it even the end of the story.

If life and death existed side by side, so did rich and poor. Which were we? Neither. Both. We had a half dozen servants, including one who "mowed" the lawn with scissors. But my parents never stopped working, knew no leisure, had no luxuries. We were like millionaires without money. When my older brother, Robert, went away to school in Shanghai, my father, realizing that haircuts cost money in the city, prudently shaved off all Robert's hair, to save twenty-five cents. (It earned my brother the unfortunate nickname "Sing-Sing," after shaved-headed convicts in that penitentiary.)

The elements were our neighbors. If we had water, it was because my father dug a well. Having grown up on a Missouri farm, my father had learned to raise, tend, and build everything needed, and he continued to so in Dzang Zok. We had to boil the well water for twenty minutes and then filter it though a cloth before we drank it. If we tasted sweetness, it was because my father kept honeybees. If we could read and write, it was because my mother taught us how. Children in America at that time, after the Lindbergh kidnapping, feared suspicious-looking strangers. My fears were more basic. I feared the wild dogs in the street. (One visiting missionary advised, "Throw charcoal—not a rock—at them; bursting, it scares the curs away.") I feared cholera. Before a trip I still find myself drinking glass after glass of water: you never know—as the saying goes—where your next drink will come from. Mine was an earthy childhood, but its earth was close to heaven. Without the clutter of many things, with few distractions (no television, computer games, and so on), not hemmed in with scheduled activities, a subtle, almost transcendent sense of something else, the lovely undertone of just being, made itself felt.

In an imaginary scrapbook, as I turn again the pages of my childhood, most of the "snapshots" or memories are happy ones. And in them a lost China lives once more. I look up, transfixed, at dragon kites—six or eight round paper disks strung loosely together—undulating in the blue sky. I steal off to play as my Chinese tutor dozes off, muttering, "Write a bit more clearly." I climb into the porcelain tub and feel the delicious shock of the hot water, heated on the stove for our Saturday-night weekly baths. At Christmas I carry red paper lanterns, three on each outstretched arm, to give to father's parishioners. The lanterns have "Jesus Christ" painted in Chinese characters on one side and "Birthday" on the other. When the lanterns are delivered, we hurry to the Christmas Eve pageant in the church, where girls from my father's school sing a carol in English to impress their parents. However, Chinese children have difficulty pronouncing our *R*, so it comes out, "Ling the melly, melly Clismas bells; ling them fah and neah." It all feels so palpable, as though there were a door somewhere and I could reenter that lost world of wonder. Well, this book, I suppose, is that door.

Yet I am sometimes told (by people who were not there) that it could not have been a happy childhood. Your parents (they point out) were missionaries, blind to the indigenous culture. They were also fundamentalists, abstainers, prudes. That is partially true. I never saw my father in less than a full suit of underwear that covered every inch of his body from throat to ankles, hands excluded. My mother could not bring herself to say the Chinese word *dung*, though it does not refer to excrement. She would drop the *g,* so that no Chinese had a clue what she was talking about. And yet . . . I am tempted to respond: no one under the age of maybe a hundred—but at the youngest sixty—has any idea what it was to be a missionary then. So let me tell you what my father and mother were really like.

※ ※ ※

A slogan thrilled my father that would chill many people today. *Let Us Christianize the Whole World in One Generation* was the motto of the Christian Volunteer Movement as the twentieth century began. It stirred my father's youthful idealism. His given name was Wesley, and a more Methodist name there cannot be. Like the original John Wesley, who traveled two hundred and fifty thousand miles on horseback and delivered forty thousand sermons, establishing charities and bringing salvation to the downtrodden, my father, who bore his name, would do the same work, on a smaller scale. He, too, would glorify God and serve man, even if at first he was not sure how to.

When my father was a student at Vanderbilt University, a recruiter from the Student Volunteer Movement for Foreign Missions spoke there. The recruiter took out a pocket watch and began counting off the seconds, but what he was really counting, he said, were the souls who, second by second, were sinking into perdition. This avalanche of lost souls were the unfortunate millions in China who would never hear the word of Christ preached to them. The recruiter paused for effect and then rang out, "Who will go to Asia? Who will give all, do all, be all to save the lost souls of China?" Wesley Smith's hand shot up.

The board of missionaries assigned my father to Soochow, where he taught at the Methodist university until he learned Chinese sufficiently to do true missionary work. In 1910 in Soochow he met a young woman named Alice Longden. A missionary's daughter, Alice had grown up in China, almost next door to the Nobel Prize-winning author Pearl Buck, whose novels spelled the romance of China for my generation. Alice was then teaching young Chinese women the piano, so they could accompany the hymn singing in church—exactly as her mother had done before her. Alice was a single female Methodist in China (of which there were not many); Wesley was a single male Methodist missionary in China (of which there were not many). Methodist missionaries should not be single. Given a similar circumscribed choice, Adam and Eve had also paired off. Alice Longden and John Wesley's marriage was to have happy consequences and—to jump ahead of the story—I was the middle one, in between my older brother, Robert, and my younger brother, Walt.

Preach the gospel where it has never been heard. That idealism inspired my parents to move to missionary-less Dzang Zok, an arduous journey first by train and then by canal boat from Shanghai. My parents were so young then, the age my grandchildren are now: I marvel at their innocence, their courage. Moving to Dzang Zok cut them off from everyone who shared their heritage, removed them from anyone who could understand them, left them among people who spoke no English. And without thinking twice they decided: perfect. But what did they actually do, once in Dzang

A missionary family in China. Wesley Smith and Alice Longden Smith with their three sons—my older brother, Robert, me, and my younger brother, Walt. We look as dour as some people's image of missionaries.

Zok? The short answer is "the good." A foundling was left at their doorstep, so they started an orphanage. They saw people starving, so they started a soup kitchen. Girls received no education, so my father began a girls' school. Since they wanted their children to have smallpox vaccinations, the Chinese boys and girls should have them, too: my parents personally inoculated all the town's children, risking exposure to the disease themselves. All this was good, but for my parents there was still the greater good to do, which was preaching Christ's love and living it out in their own lives.

I didn't learn Christianity in Sunday school; I drank it in with my mother's milk. As I trundled downstairs in the morning, there would be my father warming himself by the stove, already deep in prayer. The servants would be called in for prayer. Then we sat down to breakfast and prayed some more. The Transcendent was my morning meal, we had the

In the window of a Chinese train, we look as happy as we usually were. I am eleven months in that photograph.

Eternal at lunch, and I ate a slice of the Infinite at dinner. I could no more have imagined people without religion than I could have pictured them without clothes. The mythographer Joseph Campbell, whom I got to know years later, downgraded religion to the status of a myth, to repudiate the joyless, judgmental Calvinism that had scarred his boyhood in Scotland. By contrast, for me religion reflects reality (or realities), as undeniable and essential as were my parents and the house and the meals and everything else of my childhood.

It would have been hard to separate my parents from the religion they practiced. (As a boy I could not have done so.) My father seemed to me nobility personified. My mother, on the other hand, while loving, was frivolous. Consequently I admired my father without reservation, while pitying my mother her inadequacies. This black-and-white judgment was one I held until well into my twenties, when I began to have doubts about it.

I had thought my father noble and my mother shallow because that was my father's view, and he had implanted it in my unconscious thinking. If my mother ever bought a new dress—which was very rarely—he would denounce the imprudent folly of womankind. (Her demands were so modest; all she asked for at Christmas was a blooming narcissus plant and a box of chocolate-covered peppermints.) After Mao assumed power, my mother and father, in effect exiled, came to stay with us in St. Louis. As my wife cooked dinner for seven people, my father's contribution was to comment disapprovingly. If Kendra cut off too much skin while peeling the potatoes, he would shake his head: "What men bring into the home by the shovel, women throw out by the teaspoon." When he discovered the wine and beer I had carefully hidden in the basement, he was like an Old Testament prophet thundering wrath—"To think, a son of mine!"—until Mother interrupted him: "Now, now, Wesley, times have changed. A little wine cannot. . ."

Slowly I realized that my mother was the more complete human being—though I had every reason to know it earlier. At age twelve, when I began attending the American School in Shanghai, I forged a letter from my parents saying I could attend the school dances. When Mother discovered that I was engaging in the forbidden activity, her mild response was "Dancing does seem like a healthy activity." Many years later our oldest daughter, Karen, had a child out of wedlock. This was in 1974, when single mothers were far rarer than now. She nervously wrote my mother, her grandmother, to inform her. Alice wrote Karen back so tenderly, "It is a sin to have a baby out of wedlock, but then each of us sin every day," and every word of the letter was supportive. Mother was the more complete person, because she put the other person first, before creed or ideology.

My thoughts about my father are a pendulum swinging back and forth from admiration to criticism and back again. The sheer volume of good he did—I will go to my grave having done not a fraction as much. Risking his life, when necessary, was simply part of a day's work for him. Once a flood drowned our region, a Noah's deluge turning an area as large as Kansas, Missouri, and Oklahoma combined to liquid, and during it Father was always in his tiny boat, delivering rice to the stranded victims. After Mao's revolution, my parents tried to stay on in China, despite the peril, for there was still good to do. I have before me a letter, written on onionskin paper and dated 1950, in which Father describes delivering hundreds of cups of hot milk to the children in Dzang Zok. Had he not secured milk powder and mixed it himself at the hot-water shop and fed those children, they might have starved. He believed, of course, that there was something else to give as valuable as food. Once he went off in his boat across the lake on some mission, but the lake froze over, making it impossible to get home. Yet at 10 p.m. on Saturday night an exhausted specter appeared at our door. He had walked thirty miles around the edge of a frozen lake so as not to deprive his parishioners of their Sunday service.

Father once joked about what his idea of heaven was: a baby crying in the next room would waken him in the night, and the baby would not be his. He was referring, I take it, to more than the burdens of paternity. For four decades, from 1910 to 1950, he never heard a cry—whether from his own family, a member of his congregation, or any needy person in Dzang Zok—for which he did not feel personally responsible. *The most sublime act is to set another before you,* wrote William Blake. Setting others before themselves—that, in a phrase, was my father's and mother's career.

If I took to religion like a duck to water, the most it did for my brother Walt was bore him. My brothers became good men, in the well-trodden ways of good men. I, however, wanted to soar, and the outer limits would be only the first station stop. My older brother, Robert, did go into the family business; that is, he became a minister. But every Sunday when the service was over came his real passion: to crawl under the car engine in his old overalls, all covered in oil. "When God made me a man of the cloth," Robert would say, "he got a third-rate minister and lost a first-rate mechanic." Walt went into journalism, which thrilled me: he'll go on, I assumed, to write poetry and novels and who knows what else. No, he was content to remain a journalist reporting the news. We had the same parents; why such different offspring?

I am embarrassed to know the answer. Parents aren't supposed to have a favorite child, but I was both my father's and my mother's favorite. Freud observed that a mother's favorite son (which he himself was) will enter the fray of life with greater will and self-assurance. My parents had planned to name me Wilbur (after my grandfather Wilbur Longden) but were worried that I would be called Billy, and "Billy Smith" was not suitable for the great man they envisioned me becoming. And this, too: when an infant dies (as Moreland had),

The angel who wasn't. My parents considered me angelic, *but…* Shown here in this photo with my brother Robert—you can easily tell which of us is playing up to the camera. I likewise knew how to play up to my parents, to achieve my childish ends.

the parents' affections often get displaced onto a later child. I took Moreland's place; I became the angel who can do no wrong—though I was no angel, and wrongs I did aplenty on the sly. I knew how to work my parents' favoritism to serve my selfish ends. I'd leave adorable notes scattered around the house, calculated to double their delight in me, particularly at Christmas. As Freud predicted, my time in life would be much easier than my brothers'—which now weighs heavy on my conscience.

When at age twelve I went off to boarding school at the Shanghai American School, I was ready for bigger worlds and assumed the bigger world was waiting for me. The underside of this self-confidence, however, as is often the case, was an inferiority complex. How could it not be? Unlike my American cousins whom I'd met, I was the provincial boy, underexperienced, without a clue. Besides, I was not a good student, if not plain mentally slow. When my mother left me at the Shanghai American School she told the principal, "Don't give up on Huston. He'll get it. He just needs more time."

I did get it. *It* was Shanghai—the big world! My parents had first brought me to Shanghai years before to see one of the first motion pictures commercially distributed. *The Iron Horse* shows a speeding train (the cameraman filmed it from a pit) that hurls straight at the viewer. I hid under my theater seat so as not to be crushed to death. And now I was living in that city of marvels, schoolmate to the worldly sons and daughters of diplomats, who needn't forge a signature to attend school dances. In one class we were asked what we had read over the summer. One boy said, "*Moby Dick.*" The girl next to me answered, "*War and Peace.*" I stammered, "Uh. Uh, a book called *Miss Peach.*" On weekends, when the other kids went home, I would go out into the deserted athletic field and cry. My parents; my younger brother, Walt; our servants and their children my playmates—all of them were back home, the only place I wanted to be on those first lonely weekends. But even then I was buoyed by knowing I was on my way. Way to where? Why, in only a few years it would be to America and my rendezvous with destiny.

And along the way I discovered that my classmates were not demigods in a sphere above me after all. My first roommate kept pigeons, with the corollary that pigeon shit formed the decor of our room. There was an honor society at the Shanghai American School called Tuksis. My last year there a boy approached me in the hallway and made a *T* on my forehead, indicating I had been selected to be a member. I couldn't believe it: *Little Huston Smith—a member of Tuksis!* I truly was on my way.

Launched in the great world. This picture was taken about the time I forged a note from my parents permitting their son to attend school dances at the Shanghai American School. When I arrived from Dzang Zok, life in Shanghai seemed dizzyingly big and modern; by the time I left for America, it was not big enough.

☷☷☷

In 1936, at age sixteen, I came to America to attend college, and I never looked back. My parents would stay in China for the next fifteen years and would have stayed till they died, had it been possible. It had become their adopted country, till history in the shape of the Communist Revolution exiled them from it. I'll summarize that story briefly.

As Mao swept into power in 1950, my parents decided they would remain, for they kept out of Chinese politics and were willing to work under any regime. From the first day the Communists arrived in Dzang Zok, however, their old, useful life there was obviously over. If they acknowledged a friend on the street, that friend was suspected of collaborating with the foreign imperialists. And if the friend ignored their greeting, it hurt the friendship between them. Yet that friendship was still quietly evident: the Communists pressured the townsfolk of Dzang Zok to denounce the imperialist-missionaries, but not a single person would. Nonetheless, unable to carry on their work, my parents made plans to evacuate, only to discover they couldn't. The Communists had banned foreigners from traveling without a written permit, and when my father applied for such a permit, it was denied.

Nor was that the end of the matter. A day after the Communists arrived, their commandant marched into my parents' home and announced, "This is a large house." There were four rooms downstairs and four rooms upstairs. "You move upstairs and leave the downstairs for our soldiers." That lasted for about two weeks, when the commandant reappeared. "There are only two of you," he told my parents, as if that were a capitalist crime. "You take the two back rooms upstairs and leave the front ones for our soldiers." Two more weeks passed, and my parents were living in one room with access to the bathroom.

Meanwhile time dragged on, with no exit permit. Finally the Communist authorities told my father that if he would hand over his gun he could leave. Now, my parents were pacifists and had never owned any weapon. It was a conundrum: how to hand over something one does not have? This impasse dragged on for months, until my father recalled that an Episcopalian missionary had once briefly lived in Dzang Zok and had supposedly kept a revolver in his attic. And by chance that missionary's last name was also Smith, Hollis Smith. My father reported that this other gun-owning Smith was the man the authorities were looking for, and shortly thereafter Father's exit permit appeared.

The railroad journey that took them to the port of Canton required three days, and during it my parents did not eat, knowing that the train diner was not sanitary. But there was always a steaming pot of hot tea on the ledge of their compartment, and every mile passed was a mile closer to safety. At Canton their trunk, which had been meticulously examined for contraband at every stop along the way, received its final inspection. My mother owned a handsome piece of carved jade, but to prove she was no smuggler she placed it squarely on the top garments in the trunk. The inspector waved it through, assuming since it wasn't hidden that it must be worthless. As the boat ferried my parents to Hong Kong, they saw an American flag on the tail of a plane flying overhead. That flag had never looked so good to them.

My parents felt that, with the Communist takeover and Christianity in effect banned, their life's work had gone down the drain. Recently, however, the Chinese government has permitted the practice of Christianity (and other religions), provided it is conducted by approved representatives. And the cultural ministry has expressed interest in having my book *The World's Religions* translated into Chinese. Were this to happen, and were my parents still alive, they might think their life's work had not been in vain after all: rather, the circle is coming round.

※ ※ ※

Three-quarters of a century have now passed since I left China. What has happened to Dzang Zok—to the Dzang Zok in me? O years of childhood, would you still recognize me?

A few things have happened to me between then and now: *The World's Religions* sold nearly three million copies;

Bill Moyers filmed a five-part PBS series about my thought and work; people refer to me, probably because I have been around so long, as the dean of comparative religion in this country. Bill Moyers described my career as inevitable, as something that had to happen. But really, my life since leaving China can seem chance, a fluke, a series of lucky accidents. I met Aldous Huxley, who directed me to a Hindu swami in St. Louis. The Hindu swami, both a scholar and a saint, revealed to me aspects of spirituality I had never suspected existed. Inspired by him, I decided to teach a course, for there were none being offered at the time, on world religions at Washington University. Public television was new and ravenous for programs, so they did a series based on my course, which made me a local celebrity. While filming the series I thought, This might make a book, and a book it did make, *The World's Religions*. Some—all—of this could just as easily not have happened. And could what did happen be traced back to the years in Dzang Zok anyway?

On second thought, Dzang Zok does seem fertile soil for my life to have grown out of. The town was no miniature Chinese Jerusalem, yet it was a cauldron of different faiths. I could skip a few blocks from my house and skip past half the world's major religions. Side by side they existed, Christianity and Buddhism and folk religions and other spiritual influences. Let me count them off on the fingers of one hand.

1. First there was *Christianity*. In my childhood home Christianity was indistinguishable from living. Beyond our house, Christianity was my father's church and, to a lesser extent, the girls' school and the orphanage he founded.

2. *Buddhism.* Christianity was familial and intimate, but Buddhism and Confucianism had been historical forces in Dzang Zok and had left their visible markers. Chan (Zen) Buddhism erected its first monastery in China just outside the town, and we often picnicked there. In the town's alleys and lanes old people muttered to themselves, which I dismissed as just what old people do. Later I realized that they were saying "Dharmakara," the name of a legendary monk, and that because the Buddhist saint had accumulated so much merit, simply repeating his name supposedly brought you blessings.

3. *Confucianism.* When Confucius passed through Dzang Zok, a young man emerged from bathing in the canal without a stitch of clothing on. Confucius confronted him, Was not he ashamed to appear naked before a dignitary? The youth, named Yan Hui, answered, "With the sun as my cap, the air as my clothes, and the earth as my sandals, is there need for shame?" Confucius was charmed, and the young man became Confucius's favorite disciple. Yan Hui is entombed in Dzang Zok, and so venerated is he that even during the Cultural Revolution the Red Guards would not desecrate his tomb.

4. The elusive hint and scent of *Taoism.* The Taoist classics, the Tao Te Ching and the I Ching, were not much read, not in a town whose citizenry was 80 percent illiterate. Yet a certain Taoism seeped into my bones. I have undergone a dozen internal revolutions in my life (these will form the theme of this memoir), but oddly, in a Taoist way, always without conflict or crisis of conscience. As the Taoist yin and yang complement each other, so each

new development or upheaval flowed calmly, evenly, out of the preceding stage, though outwardly it might appear its opposite.

5. Finally, on my fifth finger, I shall name the real religion of Dzang Zok. In any textbook you read that Confucianism and Taoism were the main faiths of China, but the true religion of Dzang Zok was *folk religion*. Lanes never ran straight but winding, because evil spirits have trouble turning corners. Bottles protruded from houses with their necks facing outward so that demons, whose eyesight is not good, would mistake them for cannons and flee. Such notions, if you do not understand their psychological symbolism, sound superstitious, but my definition of *superstition* is: what you yourself do not happen to believe. Later, when I became involved in Native American spirituality, I realized that Dzang Zok had prepared me for the inner validity of its different kind of wisdom.

Growing up, I envied my American cousins their sophistication, their living at the center of the center. However, for the career I was to pursue, I was the lucky one. From the very beginning, even when I was too young to think about them, I was observing and absorbing the different spiritual traditions that met unobtrusively in that quiet, forgotten place. A child under, say, three years of age, if exposed to them, will learn more than one language effortlessly. Similarly, I learned to appreciate different religions before I even knew that's what they were. In effect, I began my research on *The World's Religions* before I could read or write.

The years of childhood seemingly will never end, and then they do end. If I could return to bygone Dzang Zok for only

Funny, you don't look Chinese. Three youth of China: me with my brothers, Robert and Walt. (Several anthropologists later told me that, when seen from behind, I have a distinctive "Chinese swivel" to my walk.)

a day, I know which day I would choose. It would be a day of no significance: I must have been under six that early morning I stumbled out barefoot into our backyard. The moist dew under my feet felt fresh, exciting between my toes. Its freshness penetrated every atom in my body. The day was just dawning, the sun was coming out, cool and warmth intermingled, and I knew that everything would be just right. I use the musical term *grace notes* to describe such moments, when our perspective shifts and we suddenly glimpse perfection beyond words.

I felt that the morning's promise of goodness would last till the end of time—which has not always proved the case. Yet I am old enough now to have forgotten what went wrong and, for that matter, much of what went right. Still, if I could re-enter that morning of grace, that small boy and I would likely recognize each other. For even then that boy was learning two truths or insights in Dzang Zok that have served me well all my subsequent life. The first is that we are in good hands. The second: that in gratitude, we should help bear each other's burdens and take good care of one another. In 1935, as I packed my trunks for America, nothing would prove more durable than those two hypotheses.

2

AN AMERICAN EDUCATION

TO TRANSFORM THAT BOY DREAMILY WATCHING DRAGON
kites in China into the man in Berkeley now writing these
words, I had to experience a dozen internal revolutions, a
dozen upheavals, reversals, and renewals. I might describe
them as twelve "frontiers" I had to cross in my life to make
it, finally, *my* life. And the first frontier I crossed was, simply, into America. Nobody—not the Pilgrims at Plymouth
Rock, not Daniel Boone penetrating the virgin wilderness,
not a would-be starlet climbing off the bus in Hollywood—
could have been more excited, more hopeful than I was as the
ship from China sailed to America in the opposite direction.

Try to imagine it. Picture a hick, provincial boy enrolling
as a student at, of all places, Harvard University. Or imagine
that same youth, ambition-crazed, arriving in New York City,
where possibilities rose higher than the skyscrapers. I was that
boy. Except my New York City was Fayette, Missouri (pop-
ulation, three thousand). And my Harvard was Central College (enrollment, three hundred).

I could describe Fayette and Central Methodist College to
you, but we would be looking at them through opposite ends
of the telescope. From today's perspective you would see in

Central College—My "Harvard." Central Methodist College, as it was then, presents a nostalgic image of an innocent, bygone America. To me, though, it was as exciting as Harvard: there I learned about the life of the mind and how exhilarating it would be to live by it.

that small stone and brick college set amid sloping farmlands a Norman Rockwell picture of bygone America, quaint and nostalgic. Arriving there from China in 1935, I felt plunged headlong into a brave new world of pure modernity, at the very turning, churning hub of the universe. I had planned to become a missionary (missionaries' children studied at Central College for free) and then return to China. Within two weeks I knew that China for me was over. America, even here in Fayette, Missouri, was too heady and intoxicating. I would be staying.

Everything seemed in motion (measured by my old Dzang Zok sundial), moving at accelerating speed. The crooked me-

dieval lanes of Dzang Zok could not have accommodated an automobile, even if anyone had had one; in Fayette everyone owned a car. In Dzang Zok nobody had a telephone; in Fayette everyone was calling everyone else on theirs every few minutes with the latest update. In China to see a movie (like *The Iron Horse*) required an arduous trip to Shanghai; here in Fayette—believe it or not—a movie showed every Saturday night. The proprietor of the theater, dressed in a tuxedo, sold you a ticket at the cashier's booth, and then walked to the entrance and ceremoniously took your ticket. By the time a newspaper arrived in Dzang Zok it was old news, but in Fayette newspapers rolled off the press twice weekly! Admittedly, most news consisted of "Mr. and Mrs. Jones invited Mr. and Mrs. Williams to dinner Thursday evening. A good time was had by all." But soon the newspaper boasted a new "World Events" column, written by an up-and-coming young writer named . . . Huston Smith. I had stumbled into a world in motion, and in no time at all I was in motion myself.

A college guidance counselor cautioned me, "Don't join too many activities. Don't spread yourself too thin." Good idea. I joined the college newspaper staff (and became its editor); I became head of the pep rally; I was elected president of the freshman class (and of each subsequent class). I had ink blotters printed up: "Have a successful year with Huston Smith as president." I penned an editorial that won a state journalism prize, which led to the dean summoning me to his office. "Mr. Editor," he said, "not today and not next week and not until doomsday will you write another editorial called 'Central College Faces Syphilis.'" Tuition was free, and I earned free room serving as the dorm supervisor and earned free board by opening the dining hall at 6:30 a.m. and busing tables. During summer vacation, I earned my keep as the traveling minister to three or four rural churches. I would hitchhike to each one, deliver a sermon, and in return receive the meager offerings from the collection plate. I am a little embarrassed now by how popular I was then, singing and ringing from the pulpit about the lost souls in China. Time itself seemed fuller then, with enough hours in the day to do anything one thought of and then go on and do something else.

But what about the actual education—the courses and classes and teaching—which was, after all, why I was there? Perhaps the less said, the better. In contrast to Central College in the 1930s, universities now offer infinitely enriched curricula. Yet I could almost pity the all-but-nameless students all but anonymous at today's vast mega-universities. At Central the professors lived across the street from the campus; we were always in and out of their houses; they were like our friends. And for an education all it takes is one great teacher, and I had that great teacher.

Edwin Ruthven Walker was charismatic, handsome, hardly much older than we were, and born to teach. I took his freshman course in Christianity and then made sure to take every other course he offered. All my other Christian preceptors told me what to believe; Walker showed me how to think. And at one thing he was brilliant beyond measure: encouraging

Huston Smith

STUDENT BODY
PRESIDENT

SHOWING SLENDER "SPEED" SMITH SPRINTING IN AN AMBITIOUS ATTEMPT TO
OVERCOME HIS ETERNAL ENEMY, THE NOISELESS FOOT OF FATHER TIME.

It is truly inspiring to see any individual face an opportunity or a task and take full advantage of the situation. Huston has repeatedly applied his talents to the advantage of the student body and other persons before even considering himself. Certainly he has been confronted with many tasks as class president for three years, editor of the **Collegian**, and Student Body President this year. Did you know that Huston writes "The Eagle Eye"?

LEADER ★ FRIEND ★ ADMINISTRATOR ★ BACKER ★ FELLO\

Page 144

BMOC (Big Man on Campus). At Central College I was president of my freshman class, and of my sophomore, and of my junior and my senior, and then president of the student body. I was head of the pep rally and editor of the student paper. The days were not long enough, and there could never be too much to do.

students. One day he came into the class and announced, "Last night I read three sentences that were as significant as any three sentences I have ever read." He then proceeded to read them to the class. They were—they were from my essay! Not a word did I hear after that. When the bell rang, I stepped out onto grass that had never looked so green, under a sky that had never been bluer, and the air hummed with excitement. Had I died then and there, I would have thought: I have had my allotment of earthly happiness.

Remember, I'd always been considered intellectually backward, academically not quite up to snuff. My mind does work slowly, but probably it has helped me be a better teacher. Often at lectures I hear a torrent of incomprehensible words coming at me like machine-gun fire. It has made me conscious, when I am the one lecturing, not just of what I am saying but of how those listening are hearing it. Were I growing up today, I might be diagnosed as dyslexic, as having ADD, or with some other incapacitating label. At Central, with a teacher like Walker, the mental cloudiness was clearing. A poem I wrote, "Semantics" (printed in a booklet of Central College student writings), conveys my sense of my intellectual awakening. The first lines go:

> Some day I intend to invent a wonderful language,
> Completely useless for conversational purpose it is true,
> But one that will give me infinite satisfaction,
> Like staying in bed for those five luxurious minutes
>   after the
> alarm clock goes off.
> I will work hard at this language until I know
> exactly what each word means.

The words will not sound foreign, like *soufflé*,
but their meanings will be strange.
After many years of labor I will be able to tell you
exactly what the word *soul* means.

Taken literally, the poem is a young man's proud dreams of vainglory. Symbolically, though, it hints that I might come into my own and the world become demystified and comprehensible.

And then one unforgettable night it did happen. The blinders fell away; I saw clearly for the first time. Professor Walker had formed an honor society that met monthly, when we would discuss a paper one of us had written on philosophy or religion. Promptly at ten o'clock cherry pie à la mode would be served, and afterward we would head back to our dormitory. That evening the discussion had been particularly exciting, and we continued our debate as we walked to the dormitory. Three or four of us lingered in the hallway, still unable to call a halt, until we remembered how early morning classes were. I went into my room and turned off the light, but my mind kept churning. Suddenly, it seemed to detonate, shattering mental blockades. I felt I had been catapulted into a fourth dimension, where ideas were the most real entities in the world. They appeared to hover in the air, like subtle spiritual energy. Plato described ordinary life as unthinking, lived in a dim cave of shadowy reflections, but said that it is possible to leave the cave and see things in sunlit clarity as they actually are. That night it felt like I was emerging from the cave of shadows. Waves of ideas—ideas that did not reflect but *were* reality—washed over me and revealed their meaning. That night changed me, forever.

I had, since arriving at Central, already changed my career goal from missionary to minister. That next morning I awoke (if I had slept at all) with a new vocation: college professor. Being a professor would allow me the maximum time to think, to discover the truth of ideas. My parents, although intelligent, had always lived by the rule, by the book; now I saw that a person might live thinking it through for himself. And thus I cross the second great frontier of my life: into the country of the mind.

⁂

Nineteen forty. The start of a new decade. I was twenty-one and had just graduated Central College, fired up with a new ambition. Fayette had gone in my eyes from a Missouri New York City to the small town it was. I was ready for a bigger apple.

Without proselytizing, Edwin Walker had in effect "converted" me to a different Christianity from my parents', so different that some might dismiss it as hardly worthy of the name. Walker's "naturalistic theism" attracted me as though through it I were entering the spirit of our time (something that, in fact, it was). "Naturalistic theism" argues that all that we can know for certain is this world, and religion thus consists of discovering and devoting our lives to the worthwhile in this world. The founder of this school of theology, and Walker's own teacher, was a man named Henry Nelson Wieman. In September of 1940 I was therefore headed for the University of Chicago's School of Divinity, then a hotbed of modernism in religious thought, to study under this Professor Wieman.

Probably few today remember Wieman, but then he was a name to contend with. He was one of a trio of figures, the other two being Teilhard de Chardin and Alfred North White-head, who attempted to reconcile Christianity with science and modernity. Martin Luther King Jr. wrote his PhD dissertation on Henry Wieman; King was inspired by Wieman's equating religion with making society on earth a more just and better place to live. Even now I find it difficult to put into words how at Chicago Wieman moved into the classroom and into our lives. When he spoke, everyone listened, even those who disagreed with him. For here was a passionate intellect who would make Truth relevant to our times.

Henry Wieman had planned to become a journalist until—almost exactly a century ago—he had a vision while sitting on the banks of the Missouri River. That vision: to uncover empirically the reality in this world that corresponds to the word *God,* and then to discover how human beings can activate that power in their own lives. After getting a PhD from Harvard, Wieman constructed a philosophy of religion that had little use for church history, biblical authority, or supernatural revelation. God, so he taught us in his graduate classes, is not a Creator but a creative process, superhuman but not supernatural. Wieman's was an unusual understanding of Christianity, in which Christ neither reformed an old religion nor created a new one: rather, Jesus was the catalyst that releases the creative powers in his disciples to transcend conventional, societal limitations. Since God enters our lives when through our creative interchanges we make history more just, Wieman became a socialist, active even in his old age, opposing the Vietnam War and campaigning for civil rights.

[35]

Wieman inspired a younger generation including Martin Luther King Jr. and, to take a more modest example, me. For years I carried in my billfold a quotation by him: "Faith is not belief but dedication to serving the highest goal you know." His admirers proclaimed how Wieman had rescued Christianity from eons of superstition. His critics charged, to the contrary, that Wieman's Christianity was not Christian or even religious. Take that quotation in my billfold: did it really require God, Christ, or even faith? However, years would pass before that thought occurred to me. When I was his student, Wieman seemed to be shedding centuries of old wives' tales and ushering us into a clean, well-lighted place of religious reasonableness. We would be the first true moderns, who would bring the deepest mysteries under scientific scrutiny and into the service of humankind. And thus at the University of Chicago, full of enthusiasm, I crossed my third major frontier: into the scientific worldview.

⌗ ⌗ ⌗

On a more personal note. I thought there was nothing better than Wieman's philosophy. But then I discovered there was something better. Wieman's daughter, Kendra. I'll keep it simple. I met, I marveled, I married.

And sixty-five years later we are still married. I knew a literary man whose wife served as his first reader, chief editor, and best critic—as Kendra has done for me. When that man finished writing his autobiography, his wife commented, "Darling, your memoir is wonderful. But tell me, did you ever marry?" (He had failed even to mention her in it.) My memoirs should not neglect to mention: I did marry. Indeed,

My teacher, my father-in-law. At the University of Chicago Henry Nelson Wieman taught me a new and different kind of Christianity. Unconcerned with otherworldly metaphysics, it had made its peace with science and was intent on improving this world. At the time I thought there was nothing better than Wieman's philosophy...and then I met his daughter.

next to being born, marrying Eleanor Kendra Wieman was the best thing I ever did. (I rank them in that order; the former was, after all, a precondition for the latter.) Kendra, the most important person in my life, deserves a chapter largely to herself: see chapter 4. But chronologically she enters the story here.

Kendra and I met at a lecture at the University of Chicago. Her obvious physical attraction only begins what was attractive about her. Never, never had I dated a woman remotely like her. Young women then, when in the company of potential sweethearts, practiced the three feminine *F*s— fawning, flattery, and flirting. But Kendra had a mind of her own: her opinions were thought out, and she stood up for them. I was intrigued, stimulated; this was better than being fussed and gushed over. (Today I still keep a pad at the dinner table, to jot down her ideas and insights.) My conversation must have made an impression on her, too, overriding my plain looks. She went home and told her sister that she had met a fascinating man. Her sister asked what he looked like. "Oh," Kendra answered, "I think he's blond." (I have, or had, black hair.) My background also worked in my favor. Were I ever to marry him, she mused, I'd probably get to go to China.

Kendra is four years younger than I am, but she was the worldly one. She wore slacks, and I was shocked then by women wearing trousers. She wore earrings, and I thought only tramps and vamps wore dangling earrings. I was mildly shocked, and in fact I needed to be shocked—shocked out of the prudishness I had inherited.

Who was this woman with whom I was to cast my lot in life? Chapter 4 will take you inside our marriage. But here's a preview. In marrying Kendra:

- I married the boss's daughter. (That joke never fails to raise her dander.)

- I married Spirit. Kendra is so naturally intuitive, practically psychic. I have studied the world's religions, while she spontaneously lives their deepest truths.

- I married the World. While I read religion and philosophy, she devours newspapers and the *Atlantic* and the *Economist* and the *New Yorker.* I married a clipping service, for she cuts out articles I should read but would never come across except for her. She worked on her first political campaign when she was eight, for FDR; last year, she was one of the first in Berkeley to wear an Obama button.

- I married a life adventure.

Last year when our second daughter, Gael, visited Germany, she encountered an actual psychic. The psychic had

Cutting the cake.
Wedding day, 1943

never met Kendra or me, but nonetheless she told Gael, "Your
parents love each other."

"Yeah," Gael replied, "married people who like each
other—that's not entirely unheard of."

"No," the psychic said, "they collaborate; they *love* each
other!"

In 1943 I married Kendra Wieman. Nine months and ten
days after our wedding I was a father. The following year I
completed my PhD. With returning soldiers attending college on the GI Bill in unprecedented numbers, I was able
to get a job as a university instructor. Everything seemed in
place. In other words, my real education was about to begin.

3

THE VOCATION
BENEATH THE CAREER

IN HIS AUTOBIOGRAPHY WILLIAM BUTLER YEATS SAID HE
had held back nothing necessary for understanding. That
raises the question, Understanding of *what*? Here, in my
story, there are two *what*s. Part one of this book relates the
key episodes that have shaped my life on this earth. Part two
then uses that life as a lens through which to view the world's
different religions.

This division corresponds to that metaphor I use for understanding human existence: the cross. Our life in historical
or chronological time, measuring and minding, cautious and
comparing, forms the horizontal arm of the cross. Our experience of the unqualified, of inner, immeasurable time (or
timelessness), is the cross's vertical pole. We live in two kinds
of time or perspective simultaneously. The horizontal and the
vertical are at once quite distinct and entirely overlapping,
and to experience their incongruity and confluence is what it
means to be human.

My life in horizontal, historical time was fairly straight-
forward. Possibly it could be summarized in one sentence:
I went into the classroom and taught. As for the details of

when and where, I taught at Denver University from 1945 to 1947; at Washington University in St. Louis from 1947 to 1958; at MIT from 1958 to 1973; at Syracuse University from 1974 to 1983; and lastly at UC Berkeley from 1983 to 1996.

I hope I was a good teacher; certainly I stinted no effort to become one. The pendulum in styles of teaching would swing wildly, from formal lectures before large classrooms (the 1950s) to desk chairs turned in intimates circles for Socratic-like discussion (the late 1960s) and then back again. Through these changing fashions I always asked myself, What makes a good teacher? After forty-plus years of teaching I can hazard an answer: the key to being a good teacher is, simply, to want to be one. And the second key: be genuinely interested in your students. Kendra's father used to tell her, "If you cannot state clearly what you are thinking, you are not thinking." Kendra appreciated, by contrast, how I would listen—with my third ear, she called it—for thoughts too embryonic or elusive for instantly clear formation. And it was with my "third ear" that I listened to what students would say, no matter how chaotic or strange it at first sounded.

In 1945, when I went to my first teaching post, at Denver University, higher education in America was about to change radically. The university had been, until then, the playground of the privileged. Under the GI Bill, returning soldiers were enrolling, and after their experience in Europe and the Pacific many wanted to learn about other cultures and other approaches. Their new young instructor at Denver University was as curious about such matters as they were.

The single most important thing I did in Denver was to leave it: I made a short trip to California, a sort of pilgrimage. To explain its origins, I need to go back to a certain night in graduate school, one that would eventually propel me across the fourth major frontier of my life.

In graduate school under Henry Wieman's tutelage, I had come to believe that we can know with certainty only what our senses report and science describes. Religion, I thought, had better face up to this fact, and the sooner it did, the better. I remember, as though it were yesterday, the night this naturalistic worldview collapsed like a house of cards.

For my doctoral dissertation I needed to discuss the philosophical understanding of pain. I went to the library and checked out three books with *pain* in their titles, and after supper I settled down to read them. Needless to say, I started with the one called *Pain, Sex and Time*, by a Gerald Heard. I couldn't stop reading that book; I stayed up all night reading it (the only time I have ever done that). When I put it down at dawn, my life was changed.

Gerald Heard may be the best-kept secret of the twentieth century. Before he immigrated to the United States in 1937, he was the science commentator for the BBC. H. G. Wells called Heard the only man he ever bothered listening to on the "wireless"; *Time* was set to do a cover story about him until the bombing of Pearl Harbor took precedence. How can I describe Heard's impact on me? If human life is considered a drama, Heard transferred that drama from amateurish high-school theatricals to a stage as large as the galaxy. What I found thrilling about *Pain, Sex and Time* was Heard's thesis that evolution was not over. We may think we are the final product of evolution, he said, but in the future human life will develop in ways beyond our present imaginings. Thus far our ever-growing individualism has utilized ever more scientific research to create endless material progress but also the endless material consumption that now threatens the very ecological existence of our very planet. That threat is severe enough to cause despair, but Heard did not despair. The curtain is now rising, he argued, on a new era of evolutionary consciousness. In the *postindividualistic* era, science and spirituality will become allies, and human beings will realize a vast potentiality now only dimly felt. A new way of understanding and living will begin.

To support his hypothesis, Heard needed an energy source to fuel this change, and he argued that human beings do indeed have a reservoir or surplus of energy that can be utilized for other, better purposes. His examples of that "surplus" were our heightened sensitivity to pain (no other species suffers as much as we do,) and, even more key, our exaggerated capacity for sex. In almost all species sexual biology is governed by periodicity, whereas human sexual capacity is unflagging as long as we are in our prime. Heard argued that this pent-up energy could burst through the current status quo, carrying us to further developments in evolution. This was exciting, but more exciting to me was Heard's conviction that of all people it was the mystics, with their larger vision, who foreshadowed the mutation about to occur.

When I closed his book at dawn, I made two vows. First, not to read another line by him until I had my doctoral degree firmly in hand. I was afraid I might forget my graduate studies and devote my life to sitting in meditation. My second vow was that when I did have my academic union card, I would read everything Heard had written.

Gerald Heard. A great polymath, Heard has been called "the best-kept secret of the twentieth century." His writings convinced me that rationalist materialism— what we can touch and look at—is not the whole story. At his monastery-college south of Los Angeles, as we sat overlooking the desert, he opened my eyes to more than can be seen.

I kept both vows. While living in Denver, I read all the books by him I could find. My next step, I decided, was to meet this Mr. Heard wherever he might happen to be. My letter to him care of his publisher received a quick reply. He would be happy to meet me, he said, but I might find it difficult. He was living in a monastery situated in a remote canyon, seventy miles southeast of Los Angeles.

Still in debt from graduate school, I did not own a car. So I hitchhiked from Denver to Los Angeles and then to his monastery. After supper we sat together on a large rock on the side of the canyon. So vast was his knowledge that no matter the topic, his offhand comments took me on a tour through history, literature, anthropology, mythology, and the sciences. So great was his intellectual confidence that if I disagreed with him he assumed that I was disagreeing only because he had stated his point badly, for which he would apologize. But there was nothing about which I wanted to agree or disagree with him. I simply wanted to experience the presence of this man who had revolutionized my understanding. After a while we sat in silence, gazing at the barren canyon walls. And the mute desert seemed to carry on our conversation for us.

I no longer share Gerald's view that humanity is continuing to evolve, but that is a minor point. His underlying message—that the world that we can see and touch is not all there is—is what matters to me. He encouraged me to read the mystics, for he said that they convey more truth about our universe than any writings except the Scriptures. My fourth frontier was the mystic, and Professor Wieman's student of naturalistic theology would soon count himself as one.

As I was leaving his canyon monastery, Gerald said, "Before heading back to Denver, there's somebody you might like to meet in L.A. He would like you; he likes to meet people who share our interest." With that, Gerald jotted down the man's name on a scrap of paper for me and waved me good-bye. It was Aldous Huxley!

At mid-twentieth century Aldous Huxley ranked among the century's greatest writers, so for me it was as though Gerald had said "somebody you'd like to meet" and then scribbled down the name Geoffrey Chaucer. When I later invited Huxley to give public lectures at MIT, the Boston police department had to augment its traffic-control division to handle the traffic jams that stretched from across the Charles River because of people flocking to hear him speak. Huxley, in person, was modesty itself. When after one lecture I mentioned his popularity, he dismissed it: "It's because I'm so old. I've become like Queen Anne's Cottage. If I live to be a hundred, I shall be like Stonehenge. . . . It's rather embarrassing," he added, "to have given one's entire life to pondering the human predicament and to find that in the end one has little more to say than, 'Try to be a little kinder.'" Gerald was correct: there was somebody I would like to meet.

As soon as I got back to Los Angeles I phoned the number Gerald had written down. The house-sitter told me that the Huxleys were at their hideaway in the Mojave Desert and gave me that phone number. Aldous himself answered. The next thing I knew I was on the bus to San Bernardino, keeping my eyes peeled for their cabin off the highway in the desert.

I spotted it and asked the bus driver to stop. Aldous came out to welcome me. Over tea, learning of my China background, Aldous asked if "lapsang souchong" was just a brand name or had a meaning. When I did not know, he said, "It's probably the Chinese translation of 'Lipton's.'" Before we set out for a walk in the desert, I helped his wife, Maria, sweep the sand out of their cabin and make their bed. I remember thinking, Life can only be downhill from this point on.

Aldous was a master conversationalist. His imposing height, magnificent profile, and sonorous voice all contributed to the effect, but it was the way he used words that seemed magic. His breadth of knowledge was encyclopedic. Igor Stravinsky said that knowing Huxley was like having a university available on the other end of your telephone line. Stravinsky once phoned him to ask the derivation of the word *scissors,* and Aldous answered him on the spot. When I was in restaurants with him, the surrounding tables would fall silent as their occupants strained to overhear his conversation. On our walk that day Aldous expressed his love of the emptiness of the desert. "The Nothingness of which the Desert Fathers spoke is not nothingness," he said. "The desert is, and it is in order that we may discover that God *is* by direct experience, for ourselves, that we exist."

Gerald Heard had led me to Huxley. Aldous that day pointed me to someone who would prove even more fateful for my spiritual development. "So you're moving to St. Louis to teach at Washington University," he said as we parted. "There's a first-rate swami in St. Louis." Swami? I didn't even know what the word meant. But since it was Aldous speaking, I acted as though meeting a swami had been my life's dream. On the scrap of paper where Gerald had written Aldous's name I scribbled the swami's name down: Satprakashananda. Little did I suspect then that this Satprakashananda would propel me across the fifth frontier in my life. I would leave the Christian frame of reference (but not Christianity) and move into the synoptic perspective of all religions complementary and combined. If the Bible or a psalm can be written on the head of a pin, *The World's Religion* was written, symbolically, that day on the scrap of paper with the swami's name.

Moving to a new city, starting a new job, setting up a new home, I might have misplaced or forgotten that scrap of paper. But I didn't. The very first week there I looked in the St. Louis phone directory under *S*. Well, lo and behold. When I called the number listed, I was told that the swami conducted discussions on Thursday evenings. Thursday evening a streetcar deposited me at an apartment building, where at the end of a long hall on the third floor, through a door slightly ajar,

I saw a dozen people sitting solemnly in straight chairs. It did not, to say the least, look promising.

Promptly at eight o'clock a dark-skinned man in an ochre robe took his place at the podium and began chanting—presumably it was Sanskrit—which was then followed by fifteen minutes of silent meditation. My attempt at meditation—a bust; I could not empty my mind at all. The whole affair felt a bit spooky to me. It was a wasted evening; I had obviously made a mistake.

He called us back to attention: "Tonight we are studying the *Katha Upanishad*. I will read from where we left off and then we will discuss." That was more like it. It was a Bible-study class. I relaxed in my chair, into a familiarity I had known since childhood. Afterward, as I was leaving, I bought a copy of the *Katha Upanishad*—a slim book for sale on the literature table.

That night I could not have dreamed that my next ten years would be spent practicing Hinduism. I could not have imagined that my very understanding of religion would be revolutionized. And certainly I could not have foreseen that Swami Satprakashananda would become, in many ways, the best teacher of Christianity I would ever have.

By the time I returned home, it was late. Curiosity, however, forced a peek into my new acquisition. Because of the hour I read only two pages, but I had not known that so much profundity could be packed into so few words. Yeats introduced his translations of *The Ten Principal Upanishads* by saying that the Upanishads reveal "something ancestral in ourselves" and that they "can appease a religious instinct that for the first time in our civilization demands the satisfaction of the whole man [i.e., person]." I read those two pages not only with my mind, it seemed, but with my body and my heart, and as I read, each part of me felt suffused, as though that part was its own pathway to the divine. Eastern religious texts are familiar today, but in 1947 the *Katha Upanishad* hit me like a bolt of lightning.

Needless to say, I returned to Swami Satprakashananda. His manner had the gentle sweetness of the saint. His intellect, however—crystalline and sharp—was like a sword that cut through confusions. He was a second-generation disciple of the legendary Sri Ramakrishna, the illiterate, loving mystic of nineteenth-century India whom many consider to be an avatar. Whenever Ramakrishna heard of a form of spirituality—Christianity, Islam, devotion to the monkey god Hanuman—he would practice it. Ramakrishna's approach became a model for my own attempts to understand the world's religions by actually living them.

Ramakrishna's form of Hinduism is known as Vedanta, and it is at once the least superstitious and most philosophic expression of that religion. Satprakashananda had founded the St. Louis chapter of the Vedanta Society, and I became chairman of its board. When the Vedanta Society saved enough money to buy a house, Satprakashananda located a suitable one near Washington University. Its owner, however, refused to sell it to "a colored man." St. Louis was a Jim Crow town then; newspapers wouldn't even print paid announcements of our meetings. So I bought the house incognito and the next day turned it over to the society.

To that house I would drive every Christmas, after our family celebration, to hear Swami lecture on "Jesus Christ, the Son of God." I had grown up, a missionary's child, accepting Christianity on faith; Satprakashananda showed me how to

Swami Satprakashananda. Both a scholar and a saint, he revealed to me depths in the religions that I had not suspected existed. Had it not been for him, I would have had no career in the world's religions nor have written a book of that name.

think about it. Christianity, seen from a Hindu perspective, becomes in some ways an even more admirable religion. No other religion, Satprakashananda said, presses the claim that God is love so vigorously. In Hindu terms, Christianity offers a unique path that unites *bhakti yoga* (love) with *karma yoga* (service). Once, different religions knew about each other only enough to kill or convert one another. Satprakashananda's approach suited a new era, when religions might interact positively.

My approach to Hinduism through the Vedanta Society became my model whenever I encountered a new major religion. Just as I had read the Upanishads, I would read each new religion's scriptures (the Qur'an, the Torah, and so on). Second, I would seek out its living authorities, comparable to Satprakashananda, and learn by absorbing their example. Third, I would do the ritual, the devotion, and the practices, to internalize the religion. After I had done all that, two things remained: I had to teach that religion, and I had to write about it. Thus at Washington University I offered a course practically unheard of in university curricula then: The World's Religions. I felt a compelling urge to share my discoveries, the treasures I was uncovering in each religion, in every way possible, including through writing. But here there was a drawback....

...I was not a writer. Having been considered intellectually backward growing up, I had little reason to suppose I would or could ever become one. I remember the exact moment when, to my surprise, I found out I could write. It came about this way.

Not long after I came to Washington University, Tom Hall was appointed dean of its liberal-arts faculty. Since he was a scientist, Tom applied to the Carnegie Foundation for a grant to investigate the mission of the liberal arts. Under that grant he and eight of (what he considered) the brightest junior liberal-arts faculty met every other Sunday evening to discuss books such as Newman's *Idea of a University* and Whitehead's *Aims of Education*. Tom took notes during our meetings, which he tossed into a large basket he kept by his chair. At our final meeting he called me aside: "Huston, you're a bright young whippersnapper. Instead of teaching in the summer school, you take this overflowing basket of notes and write up a coherent report, so the Carnegie Foundation won't think I wasted their money."

Me write them up? When I reported my assignment to Kendra, she waved away my misgivings. "Good!" she said. "Mexico would be the perfect place to write the report. I have always wanted to go to Mexico." That summer we piled our three children, ourselves, and the basket of notes into the VW bus, and off we went. While Kendra drove and the kids played and sang, I would sit cross-legged, balancing my Underwood on an orange crate, and type away. After we reached San Miguel de Allende I effected an improvement: the Underwood rested more firmly on a little table. San Miguel de Allende was hardly the tourist mecca it is today, with only a few gringo artists and beatnik writers. I still remember the opening line of one of their novels-in-progress: "Night was drawing its dark stocking over the abject city." It was summer, and we were in a lovely place. I told Kendra, "I don't know what's wrong with me. I just don't seem able to get into that depressed state of mind anymore." By the end of that summer I had the report written and ready for the dean to distribute copies.

Well, that was that. However, on campus one day I happened to bump into a professor of speech who said that he had been intending to contact me. He taught choral reading, and one piece his class had read aloud in chorus was taken from my report. If I was interested, he added, it was the last paragraph on page nineteen.

Max Beckmann. When I taught at Washington University, St. Louis possessed an international stir. I often saw this famous German expressionist painter, recognizable from his self-portraits—a brooding bulwark of a man, his head a massive dome—walking as though he carried the recent sorrows of Germany on his back. He never spoke to anyone, and groups of people parted before him, as a river does coming upon a bolder. I saw that the painter and painting were one.

A report intoned as music struck me as downright bizarre. When I got to my office, I pulled out the report and zeroed in on page nineteen. Not bad, I thought, not bad at all. I then thumbed through my morning mail, which contained the announcement of a new book published by Harper & Row (now HarperCollins). Hmmm. On an impulse I sent my report to them. Within the same week I received an answer: the report would have to be expanded, but a contract was enclosed. I had fantasized about writing a book, but that's what it was—a fantasy, like of climbing Mount Everest or swimming the English Channel. Now here was a contract in my hand. An assistant professor, at age twenty-eight, I published *The Purposes of Higher Education,* and some reviewers judged it superior to Harvard's "Red Book" on education.

Books had an allure to them then that is scarcely imaginable today. They were how we amused ourselves and how we

Werner Heisenberg and the nuclear era. After the dropping of the atomic bomb, the very survival of human life occupied people's minds. I invited Werner Heisenberg—author of the "uncertainty principle" who had worked on the German atomic bomb—to speak at Washington University on science and human responsibility. At a dinner members of the St. Louis Symphony played for us, and Heisenberg went up and spontaneously played with them. Bomb shelters and school air raid drills may now seem quaint fifties Americana, but the nuclear fate of this planet still hangs in the balance.

educated ourselves and how we enlarged our vision. Radio, movies, but especially the new medium of television were in the process of changing that. I had paid scant attention to early television, but, unexpectedly, it paid attention to me.

In vaudeville if you had twenty minutes of good material you could work for twenty years. TV, by contrast, devoured twenty years of material in an evening and always needed more, more, more. National Education Television, or NET (the forerunner of PBS), was ravenous for new programs. A representative from KETC, the NET station in St. Louis, asked Washington University's administration what the most popular course on campus was. They named a course called The Religions of Man.

And so for seventeen evenings in the spring of 1955 I taught my course on the world's religions not to a hundred but to a hundred thousand. (The KETC series also ran on NET stations in other cities.) On the day after the first show I was in a downtown St. Louis bookstore, where someone addressed me by name. I could not place the person; how could I be so forgetful? Then in the clothing store a salesman excitedly introduced me to the other clerks; they had been discussing last night's program. I would have liked to stay and discuss it with them, but I had a dental appointment. Arriving on time, I overheard the dentist tell a patient he'd have to stop now, for Huston Smith was here. The voice in the chair exclaimed, "You mean the man on television?" I felt like I had when Edwin Walker read my essay to the class, except now it was being read, it seemed, to the whole world. The fighter Joe Lewis said, "I have been rich and I have been poor, and believe me, rich is better." Well, I have been nobody and I have been somebody, and being somebody, it turns out, is not at all unpleasant.

Mayo Simon directed the KETC series, and before each show he would rehearse the contents with me. I'd deliver the presentation I had polished in the classroom, only to hear Mayo sigh, "That does not sound red-hot to me. Lose a TV attention for thirty seconds and you're dead. Let's have a funeral." From Mayo Simon I learned, for which I shall be forever grateful, not to speak dull academese or jargon. Because of his savvy direction, my public-television debut was a success. (As a consequence, I went on to do another NET series, *The Search for America,* in which I interviewed people like Reinhold Niebuhr and Eleanor Roosevelt about contemporary values.) Since there was a large TV audience for the world's religions, I puzzled to myself, might not there be, just possibly, a small audience for a book on the subject?

Semifamous in St. Louis. In 1955 I taught my course on world's religions not to a hundred students—but to a hundred thousand, on public television. Overnight I became a recognized figure around the city.

The World's Religions (originally titled *The Religions of Man*) was published in 1958, and the time, it turned out, was ripe for such a book. America had discarded its isolationism to become a world power, and people's curiosity was opening outward. And in the materialist and conformist 1950s many were going against the grain, searching for deeper truths to live by. The small audience I had envisioned for *The World's Religions* would become two and a half million readers. I knew I was an author when I saw the book in airports, where it sold for the astronomical price of one dollar. And thus I crossed two unforeseen frontiers—becoming a writer and becoming a public person—almost simultaneously. My life in St. Louis was taking off, with rollicking momentum.

I interviewed Eleanor Roosevelt for my public television series about America, its values and its future. Mrs. Roosevelt arrived at the studio looking utterly tired and old. However, as soon as I asked my first question, she—and the show—came electrically to life. The first words she spoke echo as pertinently today as then:

"Less than fifteen years ago the United States stood on top of the world, its reputation as unrivaled as its power.... We were almost in a position to dictate a *pax americana*. Today our security is in jeopardy and our principles on the defensive."

The Depression and World War II were trying times for America, but it made all the difference in the world to go through them with Franklin and Eleanor Roosevelt.

MY LOVE AFFAIR WITH THE WORLD

It arrived in the mail one fine morning. I opened an envelope addressed to me in an unfamiliar handwriting, and inside was an unsolicited—and entirely acceptable—proposition.

The letter was from a William Danforth. His name was not unknown to me. His was a famous Horatio Alger success story. Danforth had been a sickly farm boy in Missouri, where a teacher challenged him to become the healthiest boy in the class. He did, and after that he never stopped challenging himself. As an adult he pioneered a new industry, the commercial feed industry, and his Ralston Purina became one of the hundred biggest companies in America. His letter to me that day could hardly have been more to the point; it was a kind of *I challenge you*:

> Dear Mr. Smith:
>
> I understand that some of the religions you are teaching in your television course are in countries you have not been to. If the university would grant you a semester's leave and you added your summer vacation to it, a check to fund a round-the-world trip for you and your wife will be in the return mail.
>
> Sincerely yours,
> William H. Danforth

Did I need to think about his offer, even for a minute? Hardly. Thanks to Mr. Danforth's generosity, my travels began; and so began my love affair with the world.

What did I do in the different lands I visited? Guess. I trained with Zen *roshi*s in Japan. In India I practiced yoga with Hindu *yogis*. I whirled with the whirling dervishes in Iran. In Mexico I sweated in sweat lodges and took peyote

Through India by elephant and rickshaw (etc.). By teaching students on their academic years abroad, I got to visit India and the other countries of my imagination. I would travel all night, sleep on buses, and save the days for all there was to see and to learn.

with the Huichols. I meditated with Buddhist monks in Burma. I camped with Aborigines in Australia. I made a pilgrimage to Mount Athos, the Holy Mountain in Greece. At a holy festival on the subcontinent among the millions of devotees and naked *sadhu*s I wore only a dhoti under the blazing sun. I have taught innumerable students about world religions, but my teacher of the world's religions was the world.

I was fortunate. Much of the globe still wore its traditional robes. And Americans were—before the Vietnam War, before the Iraq wars—the darlings of everyone everywhere. On a second world trip a decade later, on which I took students for academic credit, the most treasured gift we could give was a John F. Kennedy half-dollar.

There was so much to see, not a moment to waste. My preferred mode of traveling was to go all day, and then at night,

instead of checking into a hotel, I'd board a bus to my next destination, napping with my head against the window. Once arrived in the morning I'd go all day again and again climb on a bus at night. It was an economical way to travel, saving both dollars and hours. Eventually fatigue would catch up with me, and I'd rent a hotel room and sleep and sleep. *What a pity to sleep at all,* I would think—until I met a man who never did.

When we were in England, Kendra read a newspaper article about a man who had not slept for forty-eight years. I'd like to meet that man, I thought. His village was only an hour by train from London. Eustace Burnett, whom I located in the phone directory, agreed to meet us at the village railroad station, and from there he took us to his house and told us his story. Born into a family of poor sleepers, he found his own sleep progressively decreasing until there came a night when he did not lose consciousness at all. And so again the next night and the night following, for the next sleepless, dreamless half century. He simply lay flat in bed for eight hours each night and otherwise continued his life as usual. Everyone has his cross to bear, Eustace said. He kept a telephone by his bed so neighbors troubled by insomnia could call him. To be available in this way, he said, was the one contribution he could make to the world. After that day with Eustace Burnett, I never again begrudged the fact that I had to stop what I was doing, get into bed, and go to sleep.

It was on my first waltz around the world that I met Eustace. My next global trip, in 1969–1970, I earned by conducting students who were earning academic credit. The theme of their study year abroad was "The Quest for Utopia." We visited communes in Japan, ashrams in India, kibbutzim in Israel, socialist experiments in Sweden, and workers' collectives in the Soviet Union. There was no shortage of (mis) adventures, not with thirty college students in tow. In India one student was so anxious she developed hysterical blindness. "I can't see anything," she would say matter-of-factly. "But it doesn't matter. India is so beautiful!" In Japan, investigating would-be utopias, we visited the Communist Party headquarters in Tokyo. As I was leaving, a policeman in plain dress stopped me and asked me to come with him to Shinjuku (the largest police station in the world). At Shinjuku I was grilled for hours on the assumption that I must be a spy for the Soviets. Finally I grew furious and rattled off the number of books I'd written, the awards I'd received, and the honorary degrees conferred on me. The interrogators backed down, started calling me a "National Treasure," and gave me a sumptuous book on Japanese art.

My weakness as an academic tour leader was that I could not rest until I knew that everybody in the group was pleased with whatever we were doing. The students intuited this about me and cooked up some mischief. Whenever a decision had to be made, they contrived it so that exactly 50 percent of them were for it and 50 percent against. Every time, I had—not again!—to displease or disappoint half of them. Finally I grew wise to the game, and when I called them on it, they told me that I had "Mr. Nice Guy disease."

I never expected we would find utopia, not on a planet populated by human beings. However, those thirty students were so intelligent, such good companions of the voyage. Our group grew close indeed. I took as a model the encounter groups just then coming into fashion: each week we set aside time to discuss what had happened and our experiences of it, to make sure nothing was festering under the surface. At our final meeting the question was asked, Has anyone glimpsed utopia? *Yes* was the surprising answer. Some students said that they had seen utopia, but it was not to be seen in Sweden or America or Russia; rather, it was in us. While we had discussed utopia, utopia had become the discussion itself, when thirty people had imperceptibly become one.

My "Stories of the Road" might fill a small volume. I could tell of accompanying Gandhi's spiritual heir Vinoba Bhave, "the walking saint of India," as he crossed the subcontinent on foot, persuading rich landowners to donate land to the poor. I could tell of being at Tiananmen Square that historic day in 1989 when a million student demonstrators were fired on by the army. A friend and I drove into the square with Foreign Visitors Support Student Demonstration in huge Chinese characters taped to the side of the taxi. My friend got hoisted to the top of taxi, and he shouted: "Democracy is not only for America or China. Democracy is for the

Protesting the war at home away from home. In 1969, on a study year abroad, the students and I staged a Vietnam War protest outside the U.S. embassy in Tokyo. The war in Vietnam—as the war in Iraq would do forty years later—converted pro-American sentiment worldwide into anti-American sentiment. We advised the students to diffuse any anti-American sentiment by saying, "I did not vote for this administration." Which was completely true: they were too young to vote.

entire world!" The students responded with an enthusiasm that knew no bounds.

I could tell of my beat-up old Renault breaking down in the middle of the Serengeti, where, stranded, I could have been eaten by lions. But twelve laughing Masai warriors chanced by, and they carried me *and* pushed the car to a cabin in a clearing. The cabin, temporarily vacated except for a servant, belonged, it turned out, to Louis and Mary Leakey, whose fossil discoveries had (as the press put it) "set the human race back a million years." The Leakeys are wonderful absent hosts, I thought as I stretched out on Louis's cot and proceeded to drink their whiskey.

Breakfast in utopia. The theme of our 1969–1970 year abroad was "The Quest for Utopia." Watching me eat my breakfast at a utopian community in Japan, the student photographer Carl Wiess said that seeing me eat so slowly, with undivided attention, was more educational than attending the lectures.

Farewell to utopia. At the second Japanese commune where we stayed, a game got started during the farewell party of catching small food items in our mouths. My expression is my comment on the game.

Tiananmen Square, 1989. Our private lives continuously intersect with the history of our time. Rarely was this more evident than in Tiananmen Square in 1989 when I saw a million students rise up in protest. My friend climbed atop our taxi and shouted, "Democracy is not only for America! Democracy is not only for China! Democracy is for the whole world!" The enthusiasm of the crowd knew no bounds.

For me any reason to travel, even a bad one, was a good reason to pack my bags and set off. If a place was on the map, and especially if it wasn't, I wanted to go and learn what could be learned only there. The coda to my travels could be these lovely lines by E. B. White, which were often in my mind:

> All that I hope to say in books,
> all that I ever hope to say,
> is that I love the world.

THREE FRONTIERS MORE

One reason I traveled so much was that life at home had become difficult. Or more accurately, not at home—rather, at my job, at the university. In 1958 I moved to a more prestigious university, one with an impeccable reputation. Instead of being an upward move, though, it went sideways. It was a new frontier, all right: the spiritual wilderness.

The name of the wilderness was the Massachusetts Institute of Technology. MIT had asked me to head their new philosophy department. I valued my new colleagues, but often they did not return the favor. Among analytic philosophers my humanistic approach was considered an atavistic throwback. One MIT social scientist told me, "The difference between us and you is that we count and you don't." The double entendre was clever, and painful. As for my interest in religion, some colleagues reacted as though I were wearing a loincloth and nose ring. Eastern religions, especially, were considered on a par with black magic and witchcraft. Graduate students came to MIT specifically to study with me, but they were not allowed to. My popularity among undergraduate students was taken by my colleagues as proof that I must be an inferior philosopher indeed. The administration, however, did value me, and whenever I received an offer to teach elsewhere, they would raise my salary. Thus, each year I became better off and more depressed.

My years there deepened my sympathies for those—minorities, women, gays, the politically oppressed like the Tibetans—against whom society has stacked the odds. It was, ironically, at the most privileged of places that I experienced a milder form of this discrimination. However, a concern for social justice was a frontier I had already crossed. I shall say a word here about my involvement in social causes, for without it I would have been a more one-sided person.

The tempestuous relationship of science and religion. I brought the speculative physicist David Bohm to Syracuse University, where he spoke before a crowd of eight hundred. After he covered the blackboard all the way across and up and down with indecipherable equations, I was astonished by one young man's question. "All this is interesting philosophy, Dr. Bohm, but what does it have to do with physics?" I looked at the board with incredulity: there was not one word on it. David's reply: "I don't make a distinction between the two."

As the twentieth century began, science equaled a materialistic worldview. As the twenty-first century began, the worldview of science, at least of physics and astronomy, may have traded places with that of religion. Consider Einstein's famous equation, $E = mc^2$. Nothing of matter dies but continues on in another form, elsewhere. The church divines and theologians for two thousand years have devised arguments and "proofs" of immortality but nothing to equal this.

⌗ ⌗ ⌗

My parents, although apolitical, had taught me I was here on earth to help—to help people and to help the common good, regardless of whether it appeared to concern me personally. Henry Wieman's theology mandated we make this world more fair and just. For Kendra empathy with the disadvantaged seems bred in the bone. When we went to Washington University in St. Louis it was a segregated college, and when we left, thanks in part to our efforts (excuse the boasting), it was an integrated one.

Future generations may not believe there ever was a time when two people identical in all other respects could not be

neighbors, eat in the same restaurant, or watch a movie together simply because of skin pigmentation. I found it unac-
ceptable then, when I marched on Selma and took part in the
March on Washington, where Martin Luther King's "I have
a dream" speech moved us to dream, too. Kendra and I were
charter members of the Congress of Racial Equality (CORE)
chapter in St. Louis, for which we received due recognition:
anonymous callers phoned in the middle of the night with
death threats. We were determined to end segregation in St.
Louis. Kendra would go into a lunchroom, for example, order
her meal, and when it was served wave to a black friend outside to come join her. The friend would be ordered out, and
Kendra would pay for her uneaten meal and leave with her,
but not before speaking with the manager and demanding he
explain his curious policy. Within two years restaurants in
St. Louis were integrated; swimming pools took longer, and
the university longest of all. I took it upon myself to invite
Martin Luther King to speak at Washington University. I met
Dr. King at the train station in a taxi (I wasn't going to trust
his life to *my* driving) and at the university kept the cab waiting while he spoke. King's southern mellifluousness, biblical
cadences, and moral argument left that overflowing crowd
stirred and steeled. The following year Washington University opened its door to African-American students. (In the
taxi back to the train station I was too shy to tell Dr. King
that I was the son-in-law of his dissertation subject.)

Earlier, in Denver, we had been part of a group of professors
concerned about nuclear warfare. In that group I was to learn
something about our society's bias against women. When
Kendra would make a point, the men (the group was almost
entirely male professors) waited with bored impatience till she

finished and then resumed as if nothing had been said. So Kendra and I devised a plan. At the next meeting she voiced her opinion—again to no response. I waited a few minutes and then ventured the same opinion, making the identical point. But this time everyone praised it and hailed my brilliant insight. That opened my eyes, if they needed opening (and back then every male's eyes needed opening), to the fact that women were being treated as second-class citizens.

I brag that I always considered not only my daughters but all women equal in every way. In reality I did not. For men of my generation, male superiority was too deeply ingrained. To be shaken out of one's unconscious sense of privilege is not comfortable, and that I was so shaken I have Kendra to thank. I did not even realize I was interrupting her when she would say, "Huston, I haven't finished yet." She also pointed out that I didn't listen to women students as attentively as I did male ones. I made herculean efforts to consciously correct an unconscious habit. That my women students later acknowledged how well I listened and respected them I count as one of my few unqualified successes in life.

Kendra finally convinced me that—despite its intellectual excitement—it would be masochism to return to MIT. With my interest in religion, I was my own kind of second-class citizen there. I began paying more attention to offers I received to teach elsewhere. Syracuse University in upstate New York, with its interminable winters, was hardly the most tempting. But they kept up the blandishments, they were so enthusiastic to have me there. When the dean's wife showed us around Syracuse, everything negative was presented as positive.

KENDRA: Does it snow much here in winter?

Concerned scientists, professors, citizens. After World War II, J. Robert Oppenheimer toured America to raise awareness about the perils of atomic destruction. I had lunch with him in Denver, where Kendra and I belonged to a group of professors concerned about nuclear proliferation. I was only following the injunction of the two apolitical people, Wesley and Alice Smith, who taught me to be concerned for the common good.

DEAN'S WIFE: Every day! Which is perfect. That way the old snow never gets dirty.

KENDRA: Is it cloudy, gray, and overcast a lot?

DEAN'S WIFE: All the time! Which is perfect. That way the sun on the snow isn't blinding.

Syracuse's chief attraction was that, unlike at MIT, I could teach graduate students there. I went in 1973 and left in 1983, having spent a fruitful and happy decade there.

Syracuse, we discovered, was only five miles from the Onondaga Reservation. One day I decided to drive out to the reservation, which became the first of many such drives. Thank God for those Saturdays with the Onondaga chiefs. It was there I realized that the author of *The World's Religions* should be ashamed: the book had failed even to mention Native American or any other indigenous religions. The religions treated in the book went back no more than five or six thousand years, but indigenous spirituality returns us to the predawn of history. I revised *The World's Religions,* and with the book's new concluding chapter about indigenous

Houses into homes. Wherever we lived—from a trailer in Denver to the second oldest house in the county outside Syracuse—Kendra's touch turned it into a home full of light and color and love and laughter. Her garden in Syracuse was so spectacular that passersby would stop to take pictures of the flowers—or simply to take the flowers.

faith the circle closed, ending the story of human spirituality where it began. The frontier in American history always had to do with Indians, and in a very different way my new frontier was the Native American religious outlook. (See chapter 7.) At least I shall not go to my grave guilty of having written a book about the world's religions while overlooking how and with whom they all originated.

☷ ☷ ☷

In 1983 I retired from Syracuse. *Retirement*—phooey. We moved to California, where our three daughters lived and I resumed teaching, at UC Berkeley, and continued to do so until 1996. I might still be at it, except my hearing worsened until I could not be certain what the students were saying. Now I am writing my memoirs, the book you have in your hands, and after it is finished, I have still one more book up my sleeve. Such—such is my career, to date. Stay tuned for what shall come next.

4

FAMILY: THE OPERETTA

ABOUT MOST PEOPLE WE KNOW ONLY WHAT THEY DO IN public, not what happens when they go home and shut the door. The last chapter outlined my career in the world. Now I invite you to come in and make yourself at home. You will meet a woman who has made the most remarkable life journey—Kendra. You will have delightful playmates—my three daughters. In "The Philosopher to His Mistress" the English poet laureate Robert Bridges thanks his paramour that he lives not only in the sphere of ideas. I have Kendra and my daughters to thank for keeping me grounded—physically, sensually, on the earth. When my daughters were young, on evenings when I did not teach I would go through the house ringing a Tibetan bell, a signal for play, the play, to begin.

Ah youth! Ah romance! as Conrad said. One finds one person who can truly share one's excitement, and that person for me was Kendra.

⸗ ⸗ ⸗

The stage set: our houses. I might describe, briefly, the houses you will be entering when through this chapter you visit us.

[75]

THE FOUR STAGES OF A LONG MARRIAGE

PHASE I.

Courtship, romance.
Ah youth! Ah romance! as Conrad said. One finds one person who can truly share your excitement, and that person for me was Kendra. My dream was to become a teacher, and only she knew how much it meant to me. There was a hitch, though: with my poor language skills I might never pass the foreign language examination. After my failing it several times, this German exam had us translate a passage by Paul Tillich, and I knew his theology so well I could guess what it said. When I saw my name on the Pass List (!), I ran the twelve blocks home and hugged Kendra and hugged her and hugged her. After telling her what had happened that way, I added the unnecessary explanation in words.

Our first daughter, Karen, was born nine months and a few days after our wedding—which says something about our passion but perhaps more about our ignorance of birth control. When Kendra phoned to tell me she was pregnant, I told her how much I loved her. She expressed relief that I was not angry. "I might have had something to do with it," I joked. With Karen's birth began my second love affair and the second stage of our marriage.

With the housing shortage after World War II, our first homes in Denver and also at first in St. Louis were trailers. Watch your step. When senior faculty wives visited us, they had to step daintily in their high heels through the mud, and once inside, their elegant hats collided with the diapers hanging from the washing lines. The first home we bought in St. Louis was a large, dilapidated affair, which my parents loaned us the money to buy. We had no cash left over for furniture, so we removed the backseat from the van, and *voilà!*—our couch. Living in St. Louis then were two Bauhaus artists who had fled Hitler: Max Beckmann and Werner Drewes. Drewes painted his house inside with bold and unusual colors—it became, in effect, a three-dimensional painting—which inspired Kendra to do likewise. Our walls were huge canvases—gold, scarlet, and blue; people said we should charge admission. The house had no air-conditioning, so in the hot, sultry St. Louis summers Kendra invented her own— a gin and tonic in a cold bath.

Each new house we moved into was like a new chapter in a book whose plot was unfolding. In Boston our home bordered on a pond, in which I swam every day in every season (except, of course, when it was frozen over). In winter I devised my own heating system—a bathtub full of waiting *hot* water—and I broke speed records dashing into it from the icy pond. Our home in Syracuse was an old farmhouse, surrounded by Kendra's phlox and peony gardens, which admiring strangers would stop and take pictures of (and, less admirably, take). Our last house, on Colusa Avenue in Berkeley, was smaller, but light fills its rooms, and my study gazes dreamily on Berkeley's golden hills. My most recent move, after the house on Colusa was . . . but I will save that for a later chapter.

Inside those houses, all was animation, motion, play. My daughters grew up seeing spirituality as a kind of indoor game. Sitting cross-legged in the lotus position—oh fun! When Kendra or I stood on our head in a yoga *asana*—more fun. After I returned from the Himalayas, I played over and over my scratchy recordings of Tibetan monks singing in three registers simultaneously, and my daughters alternated listening

PHASE II.

Family: The Gilbert and Sullivan Operetta. Having had such a puritanical upbringing, my true childhood began with my daughters'. When they were little, we had no extra money—Kendra made their clothes—yet we could hardly have been richer. Our home life was like a Gilbert and Sullivan operetta, music always in the air. I would compose songs, or adapt popular ones, to sing about whatever we happened to be doing. I wrote the music for our wedding and later to celebrate every event major or minor that followed. (Once in New York I was passing a music recording company. I thought, Here's the chance to make my fortune. The entire office looked with utter amazement when I went in and sang one of my compositions. The office chief dismissed it, "Too philosophical.") Our amusements were not confined to the musical. We invented our own pastimes; we delighted one another; each day was a new game. One evening, for example, every sentence said at the dinner table had to involve a cliché. That, as Kendra said, was "easier said than done."

to them with listening to the Beatles. The houses may have been physically in St. Louis and Boston, but they saw Asian artwork displayed and heard me speaking Chinese (and pretended that, as my daughters, they were half-Chinese themselves).

And in those houses two very different people, a man and a woman, learned to live with each other. Someone recently asked Kendra how long we had been married. "We have . . . ," she paused and did the math, "we have been honing each other for sixty-five years." Exactly, we were honing each other.

⊞ ⊞ ⊞

Two very different people. I had grown up in a home where religion was everything and she in one where it was the modern next-to-nothing. Shortly after we married, I went to California to research my dissertation under Stephen Pepper. I supported us by serving as the minister of a working-class church near Steinbeck's Cannery Row. Once when I was away, some parishioners, a retired merchant seaman and his wife, invited Kendra to dinner and asked her, the minister's wife, to say the grace. Awkward pause. Kendra muttered a child's prayer she remembered from when she was a little girl, but then she couldn't remember the word with which prayers end. Finally, instead of "Amen" Kendra said in desperation, "Good-bye." "Lady," the parishioner said, "would you like a drink?"

After we married, at meals the question hung unspoken in the air whether we would say grace. Not to say grace, for me then, would have been on a par with eating with my toes. After Kendra cooked our first meal, I said, "Would you, uh, would you mind if I read us a poem before we ate?" Today before meals we say *i-ta-dak-i-mas,* which is Japanese, not (as some people believe) for *bon appétit,* but for "I receive."

Yet despite my religious upbringing, Kendra may be the more "spiritual" of the two of us, without even trying to be. She remembers as a child hearing her father debating the famous and quite devout theologian Rudolf Otto (the author of *The Idea of the Holy*). Wieman's superior rhetorical skill left the older man a defeated and pathetic casualty. Watching the massacre, Kendra felt proud of her father, even while thinking, But Mr. Otto is right. The world is holy. In her local library there was only one book on Buddhism, Sir Edwin Arnold's *The Light of Asia,* and in the midst of its nineteenth-century purple poetry she had the startling recognition that she was, probably, a Buddhist.

Kendra may be the more spiritual *and* the more practical. One night when we were dating in Chicago, we foolishly went walking through Washington Park quite late. In the dark a gang approached us carrying guns, and when they realized we had no money or watches, they began kissing and fondling Kendra. I tried to reason with them: "Can't we discuss—" And a pistol smashed into my jaw, breaking it. Kendra forcibly shouted, "Let go!" and they let go. When we honeymooned at her father's vacant cabin on Lake Michigan, in the middle of the night thieves started to break in. As I lay there trembling, trying to think what to do, what to do, Kendra clutched a log from the fireplace, and, seeing her, the thieves skedaddled.

Were you to meet Kendra today, you would meet someone empathetic, astute, competent, who invariably knows the right thing to do. Had you met her as an adolescent, though, you would have met the opposite—a girl shy, unhappy, seemingly emotionally unstable. How she got from that miserable adolescent to being this remarkable and accomplished woman today is a story, and I will tell it briefly here.

If my own childhood was puritanical, nonetheless the basic goodness and happiness of it can make me nostalgic fourscore years later. *Nostalgia* for Kendra is not an option. There was no loving maternal figure to care for her and protect her, for her mother died when she was seven. Being told that her mother had died, Kendra let out a scream (and has never been able to scream since). Had she known what was in store, she should have screamed louder.

For the next few years she was raised by maiden aunts who did the best they could. But then Henry Wieman remarried. His new wife, whom he met on his infrequent trips to California, was a grande dame, or fancied she was. Regina, as she was aptly named, was self-centered, melodramatic, manipulative, and imperious. When Wieman truly got to know her—and after she got him fired from the University of Chicago by fabricating a sex scandal—he would divorce her. In the meantime, and it was a mean time, she made Kendra's life uninterrupted misery. Whatever Kendra did was wrong; whatever the stepmother's precious son from an earlier marriage did was right. When that son tried to seduce little Kendra, she dared not complain: she knew *she* would be the one blamed and punished.

Kendra was like the mistreated stepdaughter in a fairy tale. She had to scrounge for clothing, food was sometimes

Kendra (shown here on our first trip to Japan in 1957). The lovely, accomplished woman betrays little hint of the scarred childhood she had to overcome.

inadequate, and medical care was absent, when she was not forgotten entirely. Her father was a good man but lived in his head. Once on a vacation one of Kendra's sisters fell out of the car, and it was quite a while before he noticed. When the president of the University of Chicago made Regina persona non grata because of her antics, she converted the third floor of their home into an office and called herself a counseling psychologist. It was to these offices that she summoned Kendra one day for a mother-daughter heart-to-heart talk.

"Unfortunately," her stepmother began solicitously, "we are not all equally gifted physically. You are homely, and for you marriage will never be much of a likelihood." After letting that sink in, Regina continued, "Unfortunately, we are not all equally endowed mentally. You did not receive your fair share of intelligence, and attending a university will be out of the question. However, you need not worry, for I shall look after you. You had better plan on being a domestic servant, and I can get you a job this summer." Kendra was twelve at the time.

In high school Kendra's freshman class was assigned to write a twenty-page autobiographical essay. The teacher, a burly man who was also the athletic coach, asked Kendra to stay after class and then, holding her essay in hand, asked, "Did you write this? Did all this really happen?" When she matter-of-factly said yes, tears started streaming down the man's cheeks. Kendra had no idea why; to survive, she had taught herself to have no feeling. That day the school counselor telephoned Henry Wieman. "You must come in at once," he said, and specified, "*without your wife.*" During their conference, he told Wieman he must send Kendra away from home at once or else she would spend her life in the back ward of a mental hospital.

Bitter childhood experience destroys some, while others triumph in spite of it. It's hard to avoid the trite metaphor of caterpillar/butterfly, but Kendra slowly unspun the cocoon of her early pain and numbness, and she emerged. Deprived of a childhood, she has become a wonderful psychologist. Denied her emotions, she gradually became so emotionally attuned that she can seem almost psychic. Kendra is proof that a human being is more unpredictable and larger than we normally assume.

✿ ✿ ✿

A scrapbook of children's sayings. I joke that to compensate for my parents' having three sons, I had three daughters—three adorable daughters. I filled notebooks with their funny and sometimes wise sayings. In order not to try the reader's patience, I will ration myself here to one "out of the mouths of babes" per daughter. Well, maybe two.

Karen, our first beautiful daughter, grew up to be fiery and independent. Already as a teenager she asserted her independence, refusing to go to church. But those who go to church are good, those who don't are, well, the opposite of good— somewhere in my mind that thought had been planted. Her refusal to attend church or youth fellowship caused me to get angry, which was unheard of. (The only other time I remember getting angry was when a door-to-door salesman swindled Kendra.) If Karen gave up religion, I thought, morality will go next, and it did not take much imagination to wonder what would come afterward. Of course I was wrong; Karen turned out fine, better than any Sunday school could have produced. And I learned a lesson not taught in Sunday school about character and innate human decency. When our youngest daughter, Kimberly, followed in Karen's footsteps, it therefore did not faze me. After Karen married Zhenya, she converted to Judaism, and a part of my sympathies converted with her. Zhenya became my conduit into Judaism, as earlier Satprakashananda had been for me into Hinduism. Now

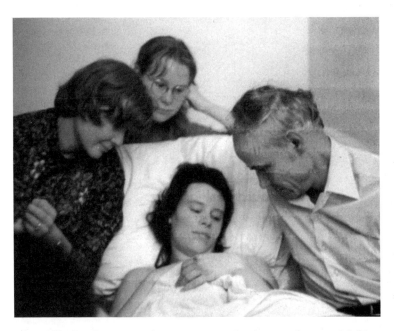

Our oldest daughter Karen, having just given birth to our first grandchild.
Kendra, Kimberly, and I form the admiring audience.

for one of little Karen's priceless sayings. When told to pick up her toys, Karen pouted, "Why do I have to do everything before I can do anything!" In my fifty years as a philosophy professor I perhaps never asked a more profound question.

Gael was our second daughter, sweet, intuitive, and with a creative turn of mind. She excelled in sports, dance, and relationships. Perhaps she did not fit the conventional mold but she found her way. In college she got a summer job at Esalen, the experimental center in Big Sur, which extended to a number of years and in effect became her "college." She became a rolfer and teaches both rolfing and continuum (a sort of sensory-awareness meditation) around the world. At times, when she is with a client she will feel a pain in her own body, and often that pain turns out to correspond to where the

*Our middle daughter,
Gael.* Here with her
daughter, Serena.

pain is in the patient's body. Now for Gael's saying. One evening when Kendra was at a meeting, I overheard Gael, all of
five, lamenting, "It's so lonesome without Mommy. I'm glad
Mommy and Daddy are not going to get unmarried. Now
we're the gayest family in the house, I mean the block."

In the delivery room when our youngest daughter, Kimberly, was born, Kendra saw—or thought she saw—a gold
aura around her. Something about her was so striking that
once a stranger stopped Kendra on the street to say, "You
know, you have a special child." Kimberly learned quickly,
and her refrain was "Want to do it myself." If you are ever in
need, I pray you may know someone like Kim. When Gael
had a serious operation and could have only one person ac-

Our youngest daughter, Kimberly

company her in the hospital, she chose Kimberly. Kendra was initially hurt that Gael had not asked her but then realized: Kim will be calm, and I would be in a panic. Kimberly's saying came from one nap time when she obviously hadn't napped at all. When I asked her if she had slept, she stopped smiling and said, "There is no answer to that question." Trying to keep a straight face, I asked, "Did you close your eyes?" "There's no answer to that question, either." And to avert further nonsense on my part, she added, "There's no answer to that *kind* of question."

Well, enough of the doting father. I was a doting father, and having children is the wonderful experience most people say it is. That is, until . . .

PHASE III.

Crisis at midmarriage. Faulkner somewhere said that you can be scared but you must never be afraid. I was scared when I got mugged in Washington Park and scared on our honeymoon when vandals broke into the cabin. But only one time have I been both scared and afraid. It was the night that Kendra said, "You know I am thinking of leaving you." I did know, but in order to keep going, I had had to suppress it. I sobbed myself to sleep that night. It is painful, even now, to admit Kendra had reasons for leaving. I am a workaholic. I can hardly wait for breakfast to be over—eating, what a waste of time—that can be better spent getting down to work. And then, too, when I was unhappy at MIT, I traveled extensively, lecturing at other colleges. There are worse kinds of infidelity than the sexual. I was living with one of the most interesting women in the world, and too often my attention was elsewhere. In *The Scarlet Letter* Hawthorne cautions us to show the world, if not our worst, at least that by which our worst can be inferred. I regret that I showed my worst to, of all people, Kendra. Fortunately, she did not leave; I attempted to make amends and began of all difficult challenges perhaps the most difficult—to actually change.

One's first child turns fifty! That age marker will give any parent pause. But when Karen was nearing fifty, she was the mother of two wonderful children, Sierra and Isaiah, and had so much to look forward to. The best time of her life, she felt, was beginning. She had a hysterectomy scheduled, but after hysterectomies women lead full lives, and Karen intended living hers to the fullest. After the surgery, however, the physician telephoned to tell her that her tests had revealed something else: "You have a rare form of sarcoma cancer and have two months to live. With chemotherapy, possibly four." Damn him, he conveyed this information *over the phone;* he could have been reporting the weather. Karen lived her remaining time heroically. She announced to us one day, "It's a red-letter day! I had a bowel movement." Her upper body wasted away, but the sarcoma tumors grew so large and concentrated—a needle could not penetrate them—that she weighed 170 pounds. Kendra told her that sometimes even while the body suffers the mind is aware of great beauty, and Karen's weak voice agreed: "Yes, that is how it is with me."

On the day before she died her husband drove her through Napa Valley: a beautiful day, the last beautiful day in the world. That night she was talking with Kendra when Zhenya told her she must get some sleep. Karen said, "But we're having such a good time!" In our last sustained conversation she told me she'd been thinking about angels. Not Christian angels, she added, but . . . she was referring to the Kabala, in which every *mitzvah* (good deed) people perform creates an "angel." Those angels don't vanish with the acts that brought them into being but live on, affecting the balance between

Our granddaughter Serena, who had every kind of loveliness and kindness a young woman may possess. Her murder left a hole in life that can never be filled.

good and evil in the world. I think of Karen's whole life as a *mitzvah* (angel), which still helps console and guide me. Her last words were "I hear the ocean. I can the smell the ocean now." Nobody wants to learn from a child how to die well, but I learned it from Karen.

The night she died, after Kendra and Gael washed her body, we remained at her bedside. As one by one people drifted out of the room to catch some sleep, I sat there alone with my daughter's body. I would sob uncontrollably, crying in anguish, and then suddenly I would feel completely calm. She's here, I sensed, not just her corpse, but *her.* The sensation was so palpable I almost turned around, expecting to see her.

After such a night, life cannot go on, but it does go on. As a boy I learned the Chinese definition of happiness: first the grandparent dies, then the parent, then the child. We had outlived that happiness. I returned to work not because my work seemed so important, but because work was the place of least pain. Kendra, more brave than I, spent a week alone in the desert, looking grief directly in the face.

There is nothing worse than losing a child; everyone says so. I said it, too: this is the worst. And then on a day I would erase and blot from the calendar—July 6, 2002—something worse did happen. As Edgar said in *King Lear*), "[T]he worst is not, / So long as we can say, 'This is the worst.'"

That Fourth of July was the last time we heard from our granddaughter Serena. Serena, who is Gael's daughter, had lived with Gael in an in-law apartment downstairs from Kendra and me: we were very close. Hers was every kind of loveliness that a young woman can possess. Physically, she was so beautiful that modeling-agency reps stopped her on the street, and the performer Prince picked her out of a crowd and became a friend. Emotionally she was lovelier yet: young or old, acclaimed or unknown, rich or poor made no difference to her, as she drew everyone out and made them feel better. At first we did not worry when we did not hear from her, because she was sailing in the South Pacific where there'd be no way to call. But the days became weeks and the weeks became a month, and still there was no news.

For some years Serena had had an on-again off-again relationship with Bison Dele, an extraordinarily talented young basketball star. Bison walked away from a thirty-five-million-dollar NBA basketball contract because his interests were broader and more intellectual, and in 2001 he was sailing in the South Pacific on his fifty-five-foot catamaran, contemplating what to do with his life. After the 9/11 World Trade Center bombings, he called Serena in New York to make sure she was OK, and he then invited her join him. She vacillated between caution and Love, but in the end Love won. The weekly e-mails and phone calls Serena had been sending all through that spring of 2002 to her mother and friends inexplicably stopped in early July.

In September the FBI was alerted when Bison's brother Miles attempted to obtain $152,000 in gold from an Arizona gold dealer under his brother's name, using Bison's passport as identification. Bison's friend and manager flew out to Phoenix to speak to Miles. Miles kept changing his story about what happened on the boat but finally said: "If you want the truth, follow me to Mexico. They don't have the death penalty there." Indeed Miles fled to Mexico, first telling his mother that he would rather die than go to jail.

In the following weeks major news organizations from *America's Most Wanted* to CNN and *60 Minutes* pursued the story of the disappearance of the athletic star Bison Dele. Our sorrow and fear were thus lived out in the midst of a media circus. Not long after, Miles was found on a Mexican beach, unconscious from an overdose of insulin, and died two weeks later. We will never know what happened on that boat. We know only that four people left Tahiti on July 6 and that Miles returned alone. When the boat was found it had been scrubbed, painted, and renamed, and all personal items removed. Serena, Bison, and the boat's skipper were gone, presumably dead, their bodies thrown into the sea.

The death of a grandchild tolls louder, because the suffering is compounded. The grief we felt for Serena was mul-

PHASE IV.

A Marriage of true minds. In working with their clients, psychiatrists will sometimes divide a sheet of paper into four squares. The first square is for things only you know about yourself, while the second is for the things that others know about you as well. A third square is for qualities they see in you that you cannot see; and—the last square—is what nobody, not even you, has yet realized about you. For me, however, there exists a fifth square, another possibility: those things no one knows about me but Kendra. I reveal things to her that I would to no one else: a part of me exists only in or through her that might not exist otherwise. After all our time living together, my identity is not self-contained: I am the way I am because she is the way she is. This "marriage of true minds" Shakespeare spoke of does not occur at the wedding nuptials but after sixty-five years of wedlock we may be getting there.

There is something as important as loving the other person and that is finding her interesting. Plato compared true lovers to two halves of one egg. If Kendra and I, different as we are, were united in the same person, that person would be, I believe, a complete human being.

tiplied by our feeling Gael's grief as well, who would now never have grandchildren. At Karen's funeral both Kendra and I had spoken; at Serena's service we fell mute, in a stony realm beyond words. After Karen's death I had returned to work; after Serena's, I sat in a dark room, to which eventually I admitted a few friends, not for them to utter words of comfort—what comfort was there?—but for the mute warmth of another presence. Yet when a reporter asked me, "Have your tragedies shaken your faith in God?" I thought it a ridiculous question. What about the Holocaust and all the other catastrophes we know as history? They did not make my own loss less but kept me from imagining that I had suffered a unique vengeance that impugned the idea of God instead of making God more necessary.

Christ said, "Blessed are those that mourn." Had I been living in Jerusalem, I would have joined the mourners grieving and praying at the Wailing Wall. Suffering led the Buddha to enlightenment, and it may cause us, against our will, to grow in compassion, awareness, and possibly eventually peace. In Buddhism monks recite daily the Five Remembrances, which are: *I will lose my youth, my health, my dear ones and everything I hold dear, and finally lose life itself, by the very nature of my being human.* These are bitter reminders that the only thing that continues is the consequences of our action. The fact that all the things we hold dear and love are transient does not mean that we should love them less but— as I do Karen and Serena—love them even more. Suffering, the Buddha said, if it does not diminish love, will transport you to the farther shore.

PART 2

The Vertical Dimension

Living in Sacred Time

5

MY SOUL OF CHRISTIANITY

OF MOST THINGS THAT HAPPENED TO ME, HAD THEY NOT happened, I would still be the same person. Erase Christianity from my life, though, and you will have erased Huston Smith.

I could express my thoughts about Christianity at great length; in fact I already have. My last book, *The Soul of Christianity,* was a book written with a sense of urgency. I worried that, in the cacophony of postmodernity's conflicting battle cries, the soft voice of personal, intimate religion may be drowned. The personal religious impulse is well suggested in the title of two paintings: Gauguin's *Where Do We Come From? What Are We? Where Are We Going?* and de Chirico's *Nostalgia of the Infinite.* They speak to the universal longing, which one has simply because one is human, for release from mundane existence with all its confining limitations. The good news, reported in *The Soul of Christianity* and indeed by any authentic religion, is that that longing need not go unfulfilled. I won't attempt to compress that book into a chapter here, but for those interested in Christianity, and who might like to hear me go on about my religion of origin, may I immodestly suggest you take a look at it?

Christianity seems practically imprinted in my genes. My earliest memories are of swelling with pride, as I listened to my father deliver sermons on Sunday—even as I found his pronunciation of Chinese faulty. Soon I was emulating him. I knew I wasn't quite ready to become a preacher. So I converted our tool room into a classroom where I became the teacher, teaching the Chinese children of the neighborhood the nothing I knew. From then to now I never stopped preaching, though at my various universities the sermons were called lectures. My summer job in college was as a circuit minister to four rural churches. I am embarrassed now to have been such a hit then, preaching about the lost heathen souls in China. In the years to come I was to become something of a heathen myself—that is, I became a Vedantist, a Buddhist, and a Sufi—but I never canceled my subscription to Christianity. Today osteoporosis makes getting to church hard, the church pews harder, and hardest is standing during the service. Otherwise Sundays might find me at either the Methodist church here in Berkeley or the Russian Orthodox service in San Anselmo or, if one could be in two places simultaneously, at both. Those churches are located in the Bay Area, but there's an invisible church I do attend, which is the Christianity I drank in with my mother's milk and which is now in the very air I breathe.

I have the perfect image of faith. My maternal grandfather was a missionary in China when warlords terrorized the country and robbers roamed the land. Bands of brigands had surrounded his missionary compound, and everyone inside the compound knew they might die. Instead of panicking or hiding, my grandfather closed his eyes and prayed, undisturbed, with perfect trust, as though he were in a mountain fortress safe from all harm. Death was of such puny consequence next to his great faith that it had forfeited its power over him.

My other grandfather, my father's father, showed faith in a different light. He died before we his grandchildren were born; to us he was only a bearded daguerreotype in a frame, who lived long ago, practically before time began. Much later, when I was teaching at Washington University, I was invited to give a lecture in Fulton, Missouri. Afterward two women from the audience introduced themselves and confided they had known my grandfather. I corrected them: my grandfather had died too young for them to have known him (although where he died I was not sure of). But I was wrong; the truth had been kept from me. He had only recently died, in the state mental hospital there in Fulton, where the two old ladies would visit him. His manic-depressive psychosis manifested, in part, as an excess. In midlife he had (as the saying went) "got religion," and whenever there was a revival or camp meeting, no matter how pressing work on the farm was, he would hitch up the horse and gallop off for it. At these revivals the saved and the to-be-saved would converge in wagons loaded with blankets and provisions, to spend two or three weeks in each other's company and in the better company of God. Back at the farm, my aunts milked the cows and fed the chickens, but the heavy work like plowing was too much for them. With my grandfather too busy with Salvation to save the farm, it would have been foreclosed had not my father and his missionary sister in Korea pooled their meager resources to pay the mortgage. Learning of my grandfather's religious mania and his being locked away for it, I worried: would, could this happen to me?

I wonder: how many sentences can I begin, "I must be one of the last people alive who can remember…"? For instance, I remember attending the founding of the United Nations in San Francisco sixty-five years ago, when I was in California working on my dissertation. And surely I am one of the few remaining who attended a camp revival meeting and got there by horse and buggy. When I was six years old my family had missionary furlough, and we spent it on the Missouri farm. In summertime, when the corn was knee-high and harvesting lay comfortably off in the future, evangelical leaders toured the American heartland. Yes, July was the month for religion. Every afternoon my father would harness Bell and Trot, the farm horses, and off we'd trot to the camp meeting. (During our next missionary furlough, when I was thirteen, we advanced to gravel roads and a Model T Ford.) At those meetings the women were like a meadow of flowers in colorful "Sunday best" dresses, and despite Missouri's scorchingly humid summer, men wore ties and jackets. As we approached the meeting our anticipation mounted, for we were on our way to meet God. I want to tell you again, folks, in July religion in the heartland grew higher than the corn. The meeting would be crowded, packed. Hymnbooks were in stacks but unnecessary, for we knew our favorites by heart.

> The Master of the sea heard my despairing cry;
> From the depths he rescued me, now safe am I.
> Love lifted me, love lifted me,
> When nothing else could help, love lifted me.

As we sang, people really did feel as though their hearts were being lifted up. A brief benediction brought the meeting to a close, and in the cooling dusk we sat down to generous slices of cellar-chilled watermelon, and seeds began to splatter the grass like large black raindrops. A bit of neighborly gossip and stolen glances between the teenage boys and girls, and we were on our way home, already anticipating the next evening.

I remember a sense of goodness then as palpable as the warmth rising from the summer earth. We expected that goodness and fellowship and camp meetings would fill our days and fill them forever. Yet when I became a professor, religion among academics was not in fashion. I got several hints that my religious interest was a milder form of the insanity that sent people like my grandfather to mental hospitals. What I had thought charming was considered suspect in academe. Especially suspect was my parents' Christian triumphalism; denounced was their missionary zeal; reprehensible was their fundamentalist indifference to life's pleasures. As a consequence (so I have been told), my life has been a reaction to all that: I first rejected my parents' form of Christianity and then rejected my rejection, as I went from my father's fundamentalism to Wieman's secularism to Heard's mysticism, then escaping into Hinduism and Buddhism and Islam. Well, that's what it may look like from the outside—but not from inside. Buddhism speaks of the Middle Way, and in Christianity, too, from within, there is a supple middle way that is accommodating, unquarrelsome, untroubled, and which makes jagged edges smooth.

My parents' Christianity was, to my boyhood eyes, neither "missionary" nor "triumphal" nor "fundamentalist." It was, simply, goodness, and as a boy I watched the drama of what goodness can do in the world. On my last visit to my mother,

GENERATIONS OF METHODISTS

LEFT: *My great-great-grandfather Gervas Smith (1805–1885).* Religion, and life, are obviously serious business.

RIGHT: *My father, Wesley Smith.* This was taken about the time he went to China as a young missionary, determined not only to save souls but to do good in every way possible.

when she was in a nursing home, she related the sermon she had heard in church the previous Sunday. A man invited his neighbor over to see his garden, but once there the neighbor was puzzled: "I don't see any vegetables or flowers." The man: "Oh, there aren't any, but look—no weeds!" My mother commented, "I thought that was very good." I got her point: not harming another is not enough; you must actively do good and help people. And that point connects my parents' Methodism to Wieman's process theology to Heard's mysticism, for each in its own way strives to do visionary good.

The Christianity of my parents led them to do a world of good in an alien world. However, had I continued to practice it in exactly the same way when I came to America, their version of Christianity would have, in the context of the Great Depression, seemed less relevant, oblivious, indifferent. Wieman's "secular Christianity," with its concern for political and economic justice, suited the hard times of the Depression. As I mentioned, Martin Luther King wrote his PhD dissertation about my father-in-law's philosophy, and indeed civil rights seemed a natural outgrowth of Wieman's kind of Christianity. If history is the medium through which God works with us, then our responsibility is to make history more just. Gerald Heard's mysticism was not a rejection of this outlook but the plausible next step, attempting to make the sacred and our own personal history synonymous. In *Why Religion Matters* I quoted Rilke's observation that we should conceive of God not as an object but as a direction. Everyone wants for herself or himself what is better; nobody wants what's worse. And like a magnetic compass turning north, I always tried to head in the direction of the better, which is the direction to God. The surprise was that the directions that appeared to lead away from Christianity led me deeper into it.

In foreign lands, in unfamiliar locales, Christian inspiration lay in wait for me when I would turn an unexpected corner. The Christians I have most admired were often among people I met in my travels. Some, having converted, lived out

Martin Luther King, Jr. King was the great Christian inspiration for my generation, who moved us to make society more just. He wrote his dissertation about my father-in-law, and indeed civil rights embodies Henry Wieman's activist, this-worldly Christianity. I brought Dr. King to speak at Washington University, and the following year the university became integrated.

their new faith like the biblical first generation of Christ's disciples (which in a sense they were). One impoverished Christian priest in postwar Japan, barely able to eke out a living for himself, would leave pennies on a ledge for people poorer than he. Another Japanese priest, after taking the sacrament of bread and wine privately, would roll up his pant legs and go help the overworked farmers plant rice; otherwise he would count his faith hypocrisy. (I wanted to accompany him, but such was his respect for professor-scholars that he forbade it. In my stead Kendra went with him and developed quite a knack for getting the rice shoots to stick in the watery dirt.) And it was from a Hindu, Swami Satprakashananda with his Christmas talks on "Jesus Christ, the Son of God," that I received the strongest confirmation—by an outside examiner, as it were—of Jesus's divine nature.

What do I think of Jesus? If judged without imagination, Jesus fulfills the criteria of a ne'er-do-well, a failure. He was an often out-of-work carpenter, born in a stable and executed as a criminal. He never traveled farther than ninety miles from his birthplace; he owned little; he wrote nothing; and he never held a position of note. Everything he said in the Bible can be repeated in under two hours (and for two thousand years we have been repeating it). In his *Quest of the Historical Jesus,* Albert Schweitzer argued that we can know for sure only two facts about the actual Jesus. The first is that we do not know much about him. (So meager is the biographical data that some have argued that there was no such man.) Second fact: Jesus was wrong (he thought the world would end soon). That may be, but even so, I am convinced Jesus reveals to us what God is like in human form.

"When Jesus had ended these sayings, the people were astonished." So the Bible describes the effect of the Sermon on the Mount. Familiarity has worn those utterances smooth, but Huston Smith is still astonished. The beatitudes turn upside down and inside out our usual way of looking at things. C. S. Lewis commented that only one who was divine could have offered the advice he did—or else a madman. Should not we be prudent? No. Jesus advises us to give no more consideration for tomorrow than do the birds and flowers. Should not we resist evil? No. If a bully hits you in the face, let him hit you in the other cheek. Shall not good behavior be rewarded in the long run? Not necessarily. Outcasts and whores may enter the kingdom of God ahead of the perfunctorily righteous. Jesus's sayings sound like koans, not to be understood by common sense. And in the place of common sense a new vision arises.

The great changes in history occur, I believe, not through argument but through *seeing* things differently. Jesus did not tell people what to do or think but invited them to see things with new eyes or with the eyes of a child. He was confident that their conduct would then change on its own. He appealed not to their reason but to their imagination; hence his resort to parables. His teachings were true, he in effect said, not because they came from him or even from God through him, but—and here he was revolutionary for his time—because his hearer's own heart could confirm their truth. A new era in human spirituality had begun.

I have now been teaching for threescore years, during which time three questions about Christianity have repeatedly been asked of me. First question: "Professor Smith, you talk about religion as a good thing, but what about all the religious wars, Inquisitions, and persecutions. Hasn't Christianity done as much bad?" Second question: "The Resurrection? Can anyone living in the twenty-first century truly think that someone dead can become undead?" Third question: "Greek Orthodox and Mormons, Seventh-Day Adventists and Quakers, Unitarians and Roman Catholics—they hardly look like the same religion. What is the minimal requirement for being a Christian?" Whatever value my answers may have, I soon won't be around to give them, so I'd better speak up now or forever hold my peace.

First question. About the wrongs done in the name of Christianity—there is no such thing as a pretty institution. Yet without becoming an institution wedded to power, it is doubtful whether Christianity would have survived. Ramakrishna said, "Religion is like a cow. It kicks. But it gives milk, too." I always taught the good side of religion for the same reason a music instructor teaches worthwhile compositions: so we can get something valuable for ourselves out of it, and have a little joy on the side.

To me the good side of religion is good indeed. In our own time progressive Christianity is undoing centuries of injustice, redressing eras of narrow-minded wrongs. Women, minorities, gays—who were all once treated as second-class citizens or, worse, condemned—now come in as equals under the Golden Rule. The minister of my church is a lesbian, and it is a better church because of her. This more just openheartedness may not describe certain bigoted "fundamentalists," though, and were I to say, "To hell with them," it would be less a curse than a prophecy.

Second question. During our five-part television conversation, Bill Moyers asked me, "Huston, do you have a hard time with the notion of resurrection?" It would be strange if a modern mind did not have a hard time with it—hard, but not impossible. In the unlikely event anybody does not know the story of the Resurrection, it goes like this (in the moving Gospel of St. John). Mary Magdalene is alone when she discovers Jesus's tomb empty. She asks a man who she assumes is the gardener, "Sir, if thou have borne him hence, tell me

Catholic monk, intellectual, writer, and seeker. In 1968 Thomas Merton and I met at an interfaith conference in Calcutta. I confessed I had monkish leanings, but the man-woman thing was too strong for me. Referring to his monastic vows, Merton answered, "Poverty—that's a snap. Chastity a bit harder, but OK. But what is hard, hard, hard is obedience." At the conference's closing address, Merton spoke off the cuff with remarkable eloquence: "I stand before you tonight to represent the people who do not count: The poor, the poets, and monks. As long as there are people who are trying to realize the divine in themselves, there shall be hope in the world."

Afterward we flew to Delhi together. We were in high spirits and fantasized about becoming pilgrims together in Nepal. "I'll write Kendra," I said, "and if she doesn't agree I'll divorce her." "I'll write my Father Superior," Merton laughed, "and if he doesn't agree, he can defrock me." A few days later Merton was dead, in an accident in Thailand.

where thou hast laid him." When the "gardener" says her name—and this is the bolt of lightning through time—at once she knows. She reaches out to touch him, but he draws back: "*Noli me tangere* (Do not touch me)." Whether the body she did not touch was the resuscitated physical body or a more visionary body is something Christians have disputed ever since, and quite possibly it is an irrelevant question. Jesus inaugurated a new mode of being, next to which the matter of life or death was secondary. Some will not have to die, he said, to enter that kingdom. Human beings tend naturally to fear death, but (unless I deceive myself) I do not fear it. That absence of fear may date back two thousand years to

T. S. Eliot. Eliot's family had helped found Washington University. He agreed to attend the university's 75th anniversary celebration on one condition: that he take communion every morning. I drove him to the church each day and sat a few rows back, too intimidated to join him at the altar. His dry reserve disappointed those at the anniversary celebration who considered him a literary god. As I admired his poetry, though, so too I admired his devotion. But the sociopolitical implications he extrapolated from Christianity are the opposite of what I understand Christianity to be.

that moment in the garden, regardless of whether it is interpreted literally or symbolically.

Third question. What is the minimum requirement to be a Christian? If you think Jesus Christ is special, in his own category of specialness, and you feel an affinity to him, and you do not harm others consciously, you can consider yourself a Christian. Personally, I exceed that minimum, for I think Jesus was what God would be—is—in a human body. Which raises the question, Was he the only one?

Swami Satprakashananda believed that Sri Ramakrishna was divinity in human dress. Everything the saintly, illiterate Ramakrishna said made perfect sense, and everything he did had a good effect, so I will not dispute those who think him holy. Today some of my friends believe that Thich Nhat Hanh speaks with the voice of a living Buddha, and nothing he wrote, I find, refutes that possibility. Yet although I admire both men, it is Jesus who speaks to my imagination.

Imagine a man besottedly in love: he won't waste time speculating whether other women equally merit his affection. Besides, when you focus on Jesus directly (or for that matter on the Buddha, or Ramakrishna), you are in sacred vertical time; when you begin contrasting and comparing him, you are back in horizontal, historical time, which doesn't admit of human divinities in the first place.

By being both human and divine, Jesus created a new possibility: the historical dimension can become the sacred dimension. Remember, in the Bible, when Jesus would go off by himself and pray all night, consuming the night in prayer? I will tell you what I think was happening. He saturated himself in a different reality; he dunked himself, as it were, like a sponge in an ocean not of water. Thus after those nights, though he did not sleep, when he returned in the morning he was neither tired nor sleepy, for his being was renewed and otherwise. To be human and divine simultaneously is so mysterious, so incongruous a chemical compound, that probably nobody—including him (in his human aspect)—has ever understood it fully. Thus it was a real question, from a need within himself to understand, when he asked his disciples, "Who do you say that I am?"

What does Christianity mean to a ninety-year-old—to this ninety-year-old? Last year I left my lovely home and companion of sixty-five years and moved into an assisted-living residence. Such a transition no one will imagine as easy. Yet purpose is still woven into the very fabric of my days. For the last time surely, I am the youngest kid on the block— blessed with relatively better health, and feeling happier to be alive, than most other residents here. I enjoy my fellow residents; I delight in leading them in singing or in creating verse spoof-commentaries about what's happening here. And I think continually of what good I can do good for them, even if it's only moving a chair from the path of an oncoming walker. Where is Christianity in my life today? Consciously or not, it's everywhere. To borrow a medieval definition of God, it's a circle whose center is everywhere and whose circumference is nowhere. At other times, though, the spirit of Christianity becomes almost palpable, a zone of safety and nonfear around me. Twenty times a day, in my room or in the hallway, under my breath I say, "Jesus Christ, have mercy upon me." Better than any pill.

Kendra thinks that I am returning to the unquestioned Christianity of my childhood. For once she is mistaken. What were once truths to be believed have turned into psychological insights I understand. Faith has become experience and experience become comprehension. For example, when I was young, Christ's "Blessed are the poor in spirit, for they shall see God" suggested to me a heavenly welfare program for the meek. Today that saying reveals an astute insight into egotism, about how those swollen with pride or vanity cannot see anything larger than themselves. However, if I have become a child again in religious matters, I'll recall that Jesus said it is as children that we enter the kingdom of heaven. I would not mind being a child again, with childhood's freshness and wonder, and I know which child I would be. When our older daughter, Karen, was seven and Gael was four, I overheard them in their room one Sunday night when they were supposed to be asleep. Karen was whispering about us: "They talk so much about God. I don't get it." Gael said she did get it, but Karen said a little four-year-old could not possibly understand. "Oh, I do," Gael answered. "They are

saying God is everything. God is everywhere. God is in me."
I am the four-year-old who would say that. I am also this
ninety-year-old.

I had to take a lifelong tour of the world's religions in order to inhabit Christianity in the spirit it was originally
meant, in the way my four-year-old daughter understood it.
I survey that long time, and my mind settles upon that moment long ago when I was visiting Mabel Martin, my college
sweetheart, in Arkansas. We were driving down a back road
along which an old black man was slowly trudging. Against
all rules of segregation and societal convention Mabel pulled
over and said, "Sir, would you care for a ride?" How simple it
seemed to me then: whoever gives this man a ride is a Christian. How simple. And how lovely.

6

MY THREE OTHER RELIGIONS

TO DESCRIBE MY ENCOUNTERS WITH THE WORLD'S religions, I might adapt Will Rogers's famous *bon mot* thus: I never met a religion I did not like. When people hear that I practiced Hinduism unconditionally for ten years, then Buddhism for ten years, and then Islam for another ten years—all the while remaining a Christian and regularly attending a Methodist church—they assume I had a checklist and went down it checking off the major religions one by one. To the contrary. When I discovered Hinduism and saw its beauty and profundity, I intended to practice it, a faithful devotee, forever. But then when I encountered Buddhism and later Islam, and was dazzled by their heady possibilities, I had to try them on for size. They fit. The proper response to a great work of art is to enter into it as though there were nothing else in the world. The proper response to a major spiritual tradition, if you can truly see it, may be to practice it. With each new religion I entered into, I descended (or ascended?) into hidden layers within myself that, until then, I had not known were even there.

Three giants are striding the earth. One is a natural scientist, the second is a sociologist, and the third is a psychologist.

That metaphor has teased my thoughts for a long time. The natural scientist is Western civilization, which since Aristotle would apprehend "reality" by studying and measuring objective, physical phenomena. The sociologist is China, which emphasizes social arrangements: like a pebble dropped into a pond, relationships in the Chinese worldview eddy out in concentric circles—from the individual to the family to the community to the cosmos—which reflect each other in the social order. India has been the psychologist, viewing the world through the lens of "the soul": the human psyche in Hinduism and Buddhism is an immense ocean, next to which moderns like Freud seem Sunday bathers hugging the shore. Swami Satprakashananda first introduced me to Hindu psychology, and to that saintly man let me return.

I. HINDUISM

Satprakashananda was perhaps the only person I know who was truly a saint. The trouble with saints is that, in their even-handed goodness, they are difficult to evoke—unlike villains, whose dramatic treacheries give the writer a free ride. (Literature—for instance, Shakespeare—would have a dull time of it without scoundrels and ruthless bastards.)

Growing up as I had, I thought I knew something about piety; meeting Swami Satprakashananda, I realized I hadn't scratched the surface. He woke at six each morning and chanted the Vedas for four hours. Only then would he be ready for breakfast and to start the day. Through him I came to see that religious life went beyond beautiful thoughts and good deeds. The noble ideas that I read about in sacred books had in him become reflex action. What is different about

Krishnamurti, the elusive "Hindu" sage. Born a Hindu, he retained its spirit while rejecting all formal religion. Claiming there was nothing to teach, he nonetheless became a revered teacher. During an interview on TV, to every probing question I would ask him Krishnamurti invariably answered "No!" With each question the *no's* had progressively more *o's* in them.

In India I heard a seeker confess to Krishnamurti that nothing—austerities, chastity, fasts—had brought him near to Enlightenment. Krishnamurti answered matter-of-factly, "Have you noticed the sunset?"

Another time I heard Krishnamurti make the most unusual claim: he never had a thought.

him, I kept asking myself, different in the deep inner recesses of his psyche, that goodness and insight flow out of him so effortlessly?

I gained a clue one Thursday, during our weekly private tutorial, when Swami asked me, "Last night, when you were sleeping but not dreaming, was your mind aware?"

ME: "Obviously not."

SWAMI: "Oh, but you were."

ME: "If I was aware, I was not aware of being aware." Case closed.

He waved my objection aside. He said that in sleep, when we are not dreaming, the mind remains active and alert. But just as dreams are instantly forgotten, even less can this sub-terranean level of the mind's operation be retained in waking memory. Yet it is then, in dreamless sleep, that the mind is closest to divinity, and were it not for our nightly immersion in that deeper mental reality, we might go crazy. (I thought of Swami's remark later, when I met Eustace Burnett, the never-sleeper in England.)

For years Swami and I went round and round on this point, without my yielding an inch. Then I went for my semi-annual dental checkup, where my dentist condemned my wisdom teeth: "Having them out will be less a problem for you than the problem that keeping them in will cause me." For the extraction I received a general anesthesia, and in the recovery room when I awoke I exclaimed, "It is so beautiful!" I had not dreamed, but obviously my mind had been aware, aware of something beautiful. My daughter Kim had a simi-lar experience under anesthesia: upon waking she exclaimed to the nurse, "I love you!" Being a private person, she was em-barrassed to have felt propelled by whatever had happened under the anesthesia to make that statement, aloud in a pub-lic hospital setting, to whoever was there. In a lecture I de-scribed such mind-below-thought experiences, and afterward a woman in the audience told about coming to conscious-ness after a concussion, practically singing, "I am so happy! I am so happy!" Beauty—love—joy: these are attributes theo-logians use to describe the indescribable God. After my expe-rience at the dentist, I wrote to Swami that he had been right after all.

I once asked an Indian philosopher the difference between philosophy as practiced in India and as practiced in Amer-ica. "In the West you philosophize from the waking state, as though the waking state were all-important," he said. "In India we recognize four states of mind—waking, dreaming, dreamless sleep, and even a nirvanic level below that—and our philosophy tries to reflect all four." All right, I thought, but let's have some proof; show me somebody who utilized all four states and then show what difference it made. When I later read *The Gospel of Sri Ramakrishna*, about the founder of the Vedanta order, I saw that Ramakrishna had relied upon all four states of mind, and that by doing so he half-erased the difference between God and man.

Sri Ramakrishna was the great saint, and possibly more than a saint, of nineteenth-century India. He was not a great intellectual; in fact, he was illiterate. But he seemed to have access to parts of his psyche that ordinarily people never do, and this gave him extraordinary power. When he was dying, the doctor touched his throat where the cancer was, which caused him excruciating pain. Ramakrishna told the doctor to wait a moment; he shifted his consciousness and then felt no pain at all. (The next day, however, when he heard two boatmen violently arguing, he felt *their* pain so intensely he could not stop howling.)

The novelist Christopher Isherwood thought Ramakrishna shows what it's like when divinity puts on human form and walks among us on earth. When two pundits questioned Ramakrishna and then announced he was "the godhead," he replied humorously, "At least it's not a mental disease." Perhaps Ramakrishna was some sort of avatar, but what I cherish him for is his human example, showing how to appreciate different religions and to empathize with different people. My finding something valuable in what everyone says, even students espousing seeming nonsense, is but the palest reflection of the way Ramakrishna dismantled the wall separating mind from mind and person from person. And every religion he thought was a valid path to God, worth practicing. Sri Ramakrishna, in effect, wrote *The World's Religions,* except, being illiterate, he wrote it with his life.

To return to Swami Satprakashananda, I recall an evening at the Vedanta Center when he made a huge vat of rice pudding, stirring the pot for hours. During a break, a woman picked up a spoon and tasted the concoction. Now, in Hindu tradition, food that's being prepared for a *puja,* or offering, may not be tasted by anyone, not even the cook, until after it's presented to the diety. Swami saw the woman tasting it, scooted over and dumped the whole vat down the sink. The woman felt offended and said so: "I am incensed. I should walk out of here and never come back. I won't, though, because you are the holiest person I've ever met." He was the holiest person I had ever met. And he was mundane compared with Indian mystics like Sri Ramakrishna. What was the country like that could produce such spiritual paragons? During the 1950s I was practically on fire to go see for myself.

Hardly anyone I knew had been to India, but in 1957, thanks to Mr. Danforth's generosity, I was on my way there. Upon arriving, on the long ride in from the Delhi airport, I inhaled India, rising from a half million cooking fires in the dusty evening air, and I was intoxicated, hooked. Over many visits over many years, I would ask myself: "What is it that made this place, these people, so different?" while at the same time thinking, "I know them. I've always known them. A part of me has been here before." I was able to return to India when I was teaching and leading students on

In India I always felt both the strangeness of India and happily at home. Here I resemble a half-naked yogi or *saddhu,* when in fact I am merely stirring the hot cereal for the students' breakfast (on an academic year abroad in 1977).

their academic year abroad. It was always an adventure. A student might knock on my door at dawn to tell me that he was staying in India and could I please inform the university and his parents. The students showed genuine curiosity about much of India; I was ten times as eager to see *all of it.* At the southernmost tip of India, for example, lies an entirely underground temple that held services at 4 a.m. The first morning I was turned away as an infidel; the second morning, turned away as improperly attired; the third morning, I wore a dhoti and was admitted. I was not to be deterred; I had to explore everything in India, both the visible and the hidden.

In that spirit I made a pilgrimage to Vrindivan, the legendary birthplace of Krishna, the incarnation of the god Vishnu. There under a tree was a well-dressed gentleman in a suit lecturing to a group, obviously about Krishna. Our eyes connected, and I thought here was my chance to find out whether Krishna had been an actual person, or a myth shrouded in the early mists of prehistoric time.

ME: Good morning, good sir. Can you tell me when Krishna lived?
THE PANDIT: Most certainly. A long time ago.
ME: I suspected as much. But exactly how long?
THE PANDIT: Longer—longer ago.
ME: In which century would that be?
THE PANDIT: I shall tell you. A longest time ago.

The pandit was right. In India there is a sense of time that does not ticktock in tune with modern clocks, just as there is a knowledge that is not gained through science and empirical experiments. In the modern West knowledge is of objective, finite particulars in historical time. India recognizes that kind of useful information: it calls it "lower knowledge." Higher knowledge (*paravidya*) proceeds differently, or rather it doesn't proceed at all but enters history full-blown on the morning of a new creation. New epochs begin when a soul, waiting in the wings, as it were—Krishna, Jesus, the Buddha, Ramakrishna—is born, and born already wise, to impart the wisdom particularly suited to the coming era.

Christ said, "I am the Truth," but Hinduism has *truths* (plural). Coming from my Christian background, I was surprised that the single destination of sanctity could admit of so many different avenues leading to it. For each different type of person, Hinduism prescribes a different path (yoga). Here I will simply refer to four of the principal ones: (1) *Jnana* yoga tries to achieve holiness through knowledge, by which is meant not factual information but understanding or vision. (2) For *bhakti* yogis, feelings are more real than thoughts, so they approach the divine through love and devotion. (3) In *karma* yoga, salvation comes through work, but work done not for gain but for its own (or God's) sake. And finally there is (4) *royal* or *raja* yoga, comprising meditation and inward exploration. Can the four yogas ever meet, be fully combined? Probably not in the same person. Imagine Socrates and Saint Francis and Gandhi and Siddhartha Gautama meeting at some ethereal pub: they might agree on some common goal, but to reach it they would head off in different directions.

All paths are equally valid, but to my thinking one was more so. For if you don't have *jnana,* knowledge or vision, how can you even understand what yoga is, what a path is? When I made this argument, in India in 1969, my daughter Kim objected. Kim loved India for its over-the-top riot of feeling and sensory overload. In India her emotions reveled in the street dramas and extravagant displays and Technicolor texture of life. When I extolled the *jnana,* yogi (which I am), I was unintentionally discounting the *bhakti* yogi, who understands through feeling and compassion, as Kim does.

Her reaction startled me. A memory, long forgotten and walled off, came back into consciousness. "Kim, if there is one thing in my life I regret," I said to her, "it was leaving you and Karen and Gael when I went on Mr. Danforth's trip in 1957." When I received Danforth's letter, I had been terribly torn: Do I seize this opportunity and feel guilty? Or do I stay home and resent my children? Everyone told Kendra and me not to pass up such a once-in-a-lifetime chance. I arranged for another professor and his family to move into my house in St. Louis to look after our daughters, and for those seven months the two families lived amicably together. Kim would brag that her mommy and daddy were explorers, going all around the world. She was seven at the time, though, and what she really felt but could not express was: her parents had died. Now in that Indian hotel with Kim, I realized that though I may have done the right thing intellectually (*jnana,*), it was the wrong thing emotionally (*bhakti*). Understanding the four yogas allowed me finally to see that. And that understanding allowed me, in that hotel room, to apologize. When I asked her forgiveness, Kim broke down and cried. And cried. And cried. And I cried with her.

Our family, though small in number, has all four kinds of yogis in it. (There's the *jnana*, papa and the *raja* mother and the various yogini daughters.) One reason family dynamics can be difficult is that the members assume they are talking to one another, but with all of them having such fundamentally different perspectives, the words sail past each other. The intimate conversation between husband and wife or brother and sister can be as mutually incomprehensible as different foreign languages. We need the different and complementary perspectives of the various yogas—and, ideally, of all religions—not only to reach God but to reach each other.

II. BUDDHISM

Out of the Great Mother, out of the cradle of India, sprang a second world religion besides Hinduism. That religion is, of course, Buddhism. In mid-twentieth-century America few Americans stumbled into Hinduism; you had to be lucky; you had to bump into someone like Swami Satprakashananda, and there weren't many like him. By contrast, if you had any curiosity about spiritual possibilities, you did not have to search for Buddhism. It would tap you on the shoulder and say, "Hey you!"

In the 1950s Alan Watts was putting his popular introductions to Buddhism on everyone's bookshelf. Huxley commented to me about Alan Watts, "What a curious character. Half philosopher, half racetrack operator." Watts was the guru of Zen who advised everyone to meditate but did not bother to do it himself. He was, however, an excellent companion to go drinking with. And if I got tipsy, it was not from the alcohol. Watts's description of Buddhist awakening, of becoming a bodhisattva, made me drunk with the possibility of awakening myself. Siddhartha Gautama had said there is a Buddha in every grain of sand, and I reasoned that if this was true of every grain of sand, there might be a Buddha in Huston Smith, too. I would have traded my soul—except that Buddhism lacks the concept of a soul—for *satori,* for a glimpse of enlightenment. Some friends accused me of whoring after the Infinite. Well, what better whoredom is there?

Alan Watts was not, however, the man who opened the door of Buddhism for me. Watts's books were popularizations of a greater figure, and it was that man who plunged me into a decade-long search for *bodhicitta,* the mind of openness and clarity. A poem by Muriel Rukeyser records my meeting with that man, which took place, of all places, on television.

FRAGILE

I think of the image brought into my room
Of the sage and the thin young man who flickers and
  asks.

He is asking about the moment when the Buddha
Offers the lotus, a flower held out as declaration.
"Isn't that fragile?" he [the young man] asks. The sage
   answers:
"I speak to you. You speak to me. Is that fragile?"

In that flickering TV image the young man is me and the sage is Daisetsu T. Suzuki. On public television I interviewed well-known figures like Eleanor Roosevelt about the direction our society was heading. The producers decided the series should include a token Asian, some wise man from the East. I proposed D. T. Suzuki, who had introduced Zen to America. I was nervous. Suzuki was ancient, and TV production then was arduous and exhausting, shot under klieg lights as hot as the Sahara. Suzuki's companion, a Mrs. Okamura, astutely brought a futon to the studio, and in breaks between filming he would take catnaps. The old man astonished me: such an impromptu rendering of wisdom before a TV camera. I felt the curtains of truth parting, and I could imagine generations hence watching this show enthralled. At the end of that long hot day, however, the head cameraman apologized: they had forgotten to put film in the camera. Would we mind doing the whole thing over? This time, tired and fatigued, Daisetsu's brilliance was less, but, if anything, his grace and good manners were even greater. I recalled a Chinese phrase from my childhood: "Your courtesy exceeds all permissible bounds." That day I determined to go to Japan, to learn what had produced such a gentle sage.

I was to visit Japan and Daisetsu Suzuki many times there. Particularly unforgettable to me was our final visit. There he

The man who introduced Zen into America. When I interviewed D. T. Suzuki on public television, he was already ancient yet never have I heard brilliance speak so spontaneously.

was, when I got off the train, looking impossibly ancient, sunning himself on the grass, talking with an old friend, another relic of time. Mrs. Okamura explained that the two old men were deaf and each could not hear a word the other said but they enjoyed one another's company nonetheless. Mrs. Okamura told how when they had been schoolboys together, they had daydreamed about their future:

> FRIEND: Daisetsu, what shall you do when you come to manhood?
> DAISETSU: My peculiar desire is to spread Buddhism in the West. And you?
> FRIEND: I shall become a businessman. I shall prosper. I shall grow rich. And I will use that money to help you spread Buddhism in the West.

Their youthful dreams came to fruition, and that fruition is: me. Me and thousands of people like me who have benefited from Buddhism's coming to the West. I am as old now as Daisetsu was then: why don't I sit deaf and content in the sun, in the company of a friend, needing nothing more, happy in *satori?*

For in Buddhism you don't have to go to heaven to realize lasting happiness. Under our neurotic frets—this is one of the first things I learned from Daisetsu Suzuki—everyone is already enlightened. Everyone is, underneath, at heart, innately a Buddha. "If everybody's a Buddha," I have heard people object, though, "why is there so much suffering and misery and war and torture." It's undeniable: people suffer, and unjustly. Yet from the heart of the combat zone we sometimes get reports of *something else.* A former student of mine was caring for his gravely ill wife day and night, until he was so exhausted that he did not know if he was coming or going. Then, in a grocery store of all places, under the neon glare, he had the uncanny sensation that everything would be all right—indeed, that it already was. The child fiddling with the cereal boxes, a pregnant woman choosing between toothpaste brands, the carts in the aisles, the light and the air—all were exactly as they should be.

My daughter Kimberly had a similar experience. When her first husband informed her, out of the blue, that he was leaving her, she was devastated. In the night she lay awake feeling shocked beyond thought. But then she felt something like a pillar of light descending through the back of her head and down her spine, and she was filled with peace. She thought, It is all right. Hospice workers report that at the very instant of death, on most people's faces a look of sweet repose comes.

In Buddhism that luminous peace already exists within, even if obscured, as on a cloudy day the sun is there behind the clouds. You need go nowhere to find it, but, inspired by Suzuki, I made up my mind to travel to Japan, to see whether I might find it there.

With China closed to foreigners, Japan became my adopted native country. Over the course of my ten visits there Japan would advance from a black-and-white impoverished economy into rainbow prosperity: only unchanging was how I always felt happy there. Polite courtesy, reminiscent of Suzuki's, smoothed the jagged edges of every human exchange. In America people on the subways or streets look harried or hurried, as though they wished to be elsewhere; I was in a hurry, too. In Japan, I became lighthearted and content simply to live. I wonder why. For my purpose in being in Japan was anything but aimless or indolent.

I had not come to admire the cherry trees in springtime or be served sake by geishas. With *satori* in mind, I had gone to Japan to meet that stranger, my own mind. I had arranged to undergo Zen training and to do so in Kyoto at *Myoshinji sodo* ("The Monastery of the Temple of the Marvelous Mind"), which was famous, or infamous, for its strictness and discipline. I didn't have much choice; its *roshi* was one of only two Zen masters in Japan who then spoke English. A marine drill sergeant might have learned a thing or two at *Myoshinji sodo*. I was told not to distract myself by reading or writing, which was almost as habitual with me as breathing. "Suppose I have to write my mother on a matter of utter emergency?" I asked. If I must, I was told, do it in the *banjo*, or squat toilet. Literary sensibility evidently ranked low on the scheme of things here.

The *roshi* at *Myoshinji sodo* did not want spiritual sightseers, which he suspected I must be. He was training thirty monks fifteen hours a day to achieve a rarefied state of mind, and here was a Western religious tourist (he assumed) who would demand exceptions to be made in his case. In my initial interview, Goto Roshi in effect dismissed me by saying that everyone there practiced sitting in the lotus position, knowing full well that Westerners could not. As it happened, though, I could.

The previous summer, in anticipation, I had trained my long legs little by little to stretch into the shape of pretzels. When I first tried the lotus position, my knees jutted up about a foot from the floor. My desk had eight-inch legs, so I rammed a knee into the space between the floor and where the bottom drawer began. After a week of tendon stretching, I wedged a thin pamphlet over my knee to force it down farther. After a few weeks the pamphlet became a phone book. I even demonstrated the lotus position on television, which elicited this letter from one viewer:

Dear Professor Smith,

This will not be long, for I can't write well in this position.

I have my right foot in my left pocket, and my left foot pretzelled and resting on my right thigh.

My question is: how do I unwind? I am eagerly awaiting your next program.

I remembered that viewer's letter at *Myoshinji*. I had never practiced the lotus position for longer than half an hour, but at the monastery we sat for hours at a stretch (or not stretched). My legs were in physical agony. The physical pain

LEFT: At *Myoshinji sodo* monastery we were required to meditate in the lotus position. I had already demonstrated how to sit in a modified version of it for TV audiences.

BELOW: *With the Zen monks at* Myoshinji sodo *monastery.*

slowly abated over two months—and was nothing compared with my mental agony when I began the study of *koans*.

Koans are Zen riddles that you do not solve so much as step through, as through Alice's looking glass, into Mad Hatterish conundrums designed to stun rational sense and in its place induce wordless insight. Perfect, simply perfect, for driving a professor of philosophy insane. The most famous *koan* is, What is the sound of one hand clapping? (Don't try hitting one hand in the air. Do, and you'll hear the sound of one hand clapping—the *roshi*'s against the side of your head.) My *koan* concerned a monk who asked Joshu (a famous master in Tang-dynasty China), "Does a dog have a Buddha-nature?" Joshu's answer seemed to imply no. The conundrum: since the Buddha said that even the grass has Buddha-nature, how can a dog *not* have it?

Every day I came up with another ingenious answer; every day the *roshi* frowned and shook his head no; every day the bell would ring and I would be told to come back tomorrow. I turned the *koan* upside down; I pulled it inside out; I unpacked each word and repacked its meaning. Finally I thought, I've got it. The key word was *have*. A dog does not *have* Buddha-nature, not the way I have a shirt or an ice-cream cone. Rather Buddha-nature has, or is momentarily taking the shape of, that dog. But the *roshi* did not even hear out my ingenious solution. Halfway through my explanation he roared at me, "You have the philosopher's disease!" Then he softened a bit: "There's nothing wrong with philosophy. I myself have a master's degree in it from one of our better universities. Philosophy works only with reason, though, and there's nothing wrong with reason, either. Your reasoning is fine, but your experience is limited. Enlarge your experience, and your philosophy will be different." *Ding-a-ling-a-ling* sounded the little bell—signal that the interview was over. I had my impossible assignment: to think of how to think the way I do not think.

At *Myoshinji* a stick such as this was used to not-so-gently prod sleepy and sleeping meditators. After a week of our round-the-clock meditating, the supervising monk presented me this stick, inscribed: *I present this to my respected friend, Professor Smith, as a commemoration of his having spent one week hardest Zazen training called Gematsu-Ohzesshin with us at Myoshinji-sodo and you have been struck with this keisaku for encouragement of your will by me. July 26, 1957. Daijo Shiozawa.*

If a *koan* is mentally exhausting, try it on sleep depriva-tion. It all but pushed me over the edge. At the end of my stay at *Myoshinji* there was something like a final-exam pe-riod, when the monks meditated virtually around the clock. Since I was a novice, I was permitted the sybaritic luxury of three and a half hours' sleep a night, which was grossly in-sufficient. That prolonged sleep deprivation was the hardest ordeal I've ever endured. After the first night I was simply sleepy. By the third night I was a zombie. From then on it got worse. The *koans* force the rational mind to the end of its tether, and then sleep deprivation kicks in. Since you are not sleeping and hence not dreaming, you in effect dream or lapse into quasi hallucinations while you are awake, a kind of a temporary psychosis. I was in that altered state during my last days at *Myoshinji*.

And in that state I stormed into the *roshi*'s room. Self-pity had become boring; fury was the order of the day. What a way to treat human beings, I raged to myself. I wouldn't just throw in the towel, I'd smack it across the *roshi*'s face. However, a certain decorum prevailed as I entered his audience room. I clasped palms together and bowed reverentially; as I approached him I touched my head to the tatami floor mat and flexed my outreached fingers upward to symbolize lifting the dust off the Buddha's feet. Then our eyes met in a mutual glare. For a few moments he said nothing, and then he growled, "How's it going?" It sounded like a taunt.

"Terrible!" I shouted.

"You think you are going to get sick, don't you?" More taunting sarcasm, so I let him have it.

"Yes, I think I'm going to get sick! Sick because of you!" For several days my throat had begun to contract and I was having to labor to breathe.

And then, curiously, his face relaxed. His smirking expression disappeared, and with total matter-of-factness he said, "What is sickness? What is health? Put aside both and go forward."

I despair of ever conveying the uncanny impact those twelve words had on me. I thought, He's right. He is right! Sickness and health suddenly seemed beside the point of what it means to be human; compared to that more abiding reality, health and sickness were two sides of the same coin.

Buddhism speaks of the "Great No's," such as "no birth, no death" and "no coming, no going." There is something within us that is not born and does not die and that comes from nowhere and goes no place. Somehow after the *roshi's* few words I found myself unexpectedly in a state of total peace. I did my prescribed bow to the floor and exited the room, not only determined to complete the two remaining days but confident that I could do so. Since then I have often been sick, but off it goes to the side, and I go forward.

When I had been sitting contorted for hours in the lotus position, that month seemed to drag on forever; now all too quickly it was over. It was time to say good-bye. Ritual governed all aspects of life at *Myoshinji sodo*, so I knew my farewell interview with Goto Roshi would be a ceremonious and formal affair. I was wrong. Roshi met me at the doorway to his tiny house, not in his usual priestly robes but dressed casually. He could have been anybody and I somebody who just chanced to drop by. In his miniature living room he pulled back a short hanging curtain and introduced me to a shriveled-up woman working at a tiny stove. "This is *Oksan,* who takes care of my food." Then through another sawed-off curtain, he gestured to a futon on which a thin coverlet was spread. "This is my bedroom, and this is my television where I watch sumo wrestling. Do you watch sumo wrestling? Oh, too bad. It's wonderful!" He led me out the back door, where empty beer bottles were stacked. "And here are the remnants of the beer I drink while watching sumo wrestling." I got it: he was knocking the teacher off his pedestal. But then he proceeded to knock Zen off its pedestal. *Koans* can be a useful exercise, he said, but they are not Zen. And sitting in meditation, he went on—that is not Zen. Then why had I been torturing myself with *koans* and body aerobatics, I wondered, and what the hell, then, was Zen?

"You will be flying home tomorrow," he said. "Don't overlook how many people will help you to get home—ticketing agents, pilots, cabin attendants, those who prepare your meals." He bowed and placed his palms together, demonstrating *gassho,* the gesture of gratitude. Straightening up, he pointed to the beam that supported the corner of the house. Another *gassho.* He glanced up at the ceiling that kept the house dry and executed yet another *gassho.* Then he did a *gassho* to me. "Make your whole life unceasing gratitude," he said. "What is Zen? Simple, simple, so simple. Infinite gratitude toward all things past; infinite service to all things present; infinite responsibility to all things future. Have a safe journey home." And he gave me a wonderful smile. "I am glad you came."

✲ ✲ ✲

Such was my initiation into Buddhism. Each new Buddhist country I visited was like another classroom, a deeper immersion into dharma studies. In Thailand the saffron-robed monks sallied forth at dawn with their begging bowls, and Huston Smith with his begging bowl went with them. In America we would have thanked and chatted with the benefactors who put food in our bowls. Here the monks, holding out their bowls, did not look up at the women; the women, giving us our food, did not look directly at the monks. It was Goto Roshi's pure gratitude on one side and pure generosity on the other. Does a dog have Buddha-nature? Our bodies, in those moments, experienced the nature of generosity and gratitude, and we felt more alive.

In Burma, Kendra and I went on retreat with the Vipassana master U Ba Khin. The body is its own spiritual journey. When we meditated on the body, wherever Kendra focused her attention, her skin would turn red at exactly that point. During the retreat she became ill with diarrhea and vomiting, but U Ba Khin pronounced that a good sign. He hinted at possessing extraordinary powers. I gave no credence to his claim that he could cure the sick, but when U Ba Khin boasted of having a student who could go into *samadi* (that deep trance supposedly bordering on enlightenment) at will, I was intrigued. U Ba Khin summoned the student—a successful businessman who used meditation to cure his horrendous migraines—and told him to go into *samadi*. U Ba Khin then invited me: "Go ahead. You can stick him with a needle now." No thank you. However, I clapped my hands loudly next to his ears and he stirred no more than a statue, and when Kendra took his pulse, it was thirty beats per minute. The man became a celebrated meditation teacher—S. N. Goenka. Later in India, Goenka told Kendra he was planning a ten-day retreat, and he planned not to sleep at all during ten days. I was moving into things undreamed of at the University of Chicago philosophy department.

The Chinese had sealed off Tibet from foreigners, so in 1964 I traveled to the Tibetan areas of northern India to learn of their form of Buddhism. Arriving at a Tibetan monastery in the Himalayas, I was ushered into the abbot's bungalow, and a hot bowl of Tibetan tea was placed in my hands. In my travels I have encountered only two objectionable foods—

poi in Hawaii, which would make excellent wallpaper paste, and Tibetan tea. I took a big gulp before its rancid yak-butter and rock-salt taste registered. A woman missionary in Africa, when served a soup made from a live monkey thrown into a pot of boiling water, prayed, "Lord, I'll put it down, if you'll keep it down." I could see myself throwing up over the gorgeous Tibetan carpets on the floor.

I retired early, in preparation for a four-day festival that would begin at three in the morning. Three a.m. came ungodly early, and as I listened to the lamas' monotonous chanting, it was still dark outside. I was tired from my travels, and—what I'm getting around to is . . . I fell asleep. Only to be jolted awake: the monotonous monotone had changed into beautiful tonal chords. I thought I was still dreaming, surrounded by an angelic choir. The choir then stopped singing, leaving it all to a cantor. It was stranger than any dream: a first, a third, and a barely audible fifth chord came from his single larynx! Nobody in the music department at MIT, I thought, is going to believe this. I borrowed an old German tape recorder, to prove to skeptics back at MIT that the human voice can sound more than one tone at a time. As a result a new term would enter the vocabulary of musicology: *multiphonic chanting*. A second result of the scratchy tape I made is that the Grateful Dead came to hear about these monks and sponsored them on several world tours. Indeed,

OPPOSITE: *Tibetan chanting*. Philosophy professors are supposed to think and reason, not to discover things in the real world. In northern India in 1964 I make an actual discovery: Tibetan monks can sing in three chords simultaneously. It led to a new word in musicology, *multiphonic chanting*, and to the Grateful Dead's sponsoring the monks on several world tours.

Tibetan lama, with symbolic gesture, chants
solo chord. Below, Huston Smith (center) and
Irving Hartley record the phenomenon.

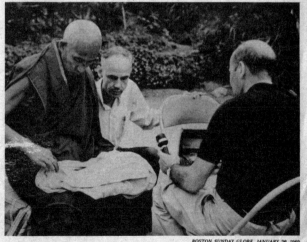

BOSTON SUNDAY GLOBE, JANUARY 26, 1969

multiphonic chanting became something of a fad; popular courses were given in it (Kendra took one), and the choir at St. John the Divine in New York began to sing it.

What those lamas did, however, has a significance that goes beyond singing. They took from the outskirts of awareness overtones ordinarily too faint to be heard and made them conscious. This is what worship is intended to do: move the sacred—in this case, sacred sound—from the periphery to the center. I asked one lama, "What's it like to sing like that?" He answered that at first it was quite ordinary, what anyone experiences when singing. Then, as the resonant chords take on a life of their own, it felt as though not he but a deity was creating the music and he was just riding the waves of it. As the chanting climaxed, in that crescendo all distinction between lama, deity, and chords collapsed and all sound was holy sound.

As I was leaving the monastery, the monks said that I should go to Dharamsala and meet the Dalai Lama. No. I would not intrude upon that busy man just to boast that I had shaken his hand. But the monks, it turned out, had already arranged the interview. I was determined to limit the meeting to ten minutes, knowing that the Dalai Lama had more important things to do. Thus it came about that a few days later I did shake his hand (a firm, warm handshake it was), and I expressed my sympathy for the Tibetan people and proposed that he visit America. He said that I was the first person to make that suggestion. I could not but be impressed: here was someone raised like a king and venerated like a god, yet he exhibited not the faintest trace of egotism. We conversed through a translator, but after ten minutes as I rose to leave, he mumbled to himself in English, "I must decide what is important. Decide now." Then he said to me, Please, would I sit down again, and could I stay longer?

It was due to a misunderstanding. On my calling card was Massachusetts Institute of Technology, and since I taught at MIT, the Dalai Lama assumed I must be a scientist. Since his arrival in the modern world only a few short years before, the new scientific theories he was hearing about, from DNA to the big bang, had intrigued him. Did they disprove Buddhism, or did they validate it? Surely a professor from MIT could answer his questions. Fortunately I had recently heard the Harvard astrophysicist Harlow Shapley lecture on the big bang, on how the universe expands and contracts—which suggests there may have been more than one big bang. The Dalai Lama concurred: "It's bang bang bang." From my explanation of DNA, he concluded that DNA was compatible with Buddhist reincarnation. "But if the words of the Buddha and the finding of modern science contradict each other," the Dalai Lama added, "the former has to go." He was not setting science above religion, but expressing his conviction that the two are allies, different roads to one reality. In *The Universe in a Single Atom: The Convergence of Science and Spirituality* he would later write: "When I count my teachers of science, I include Huston Smith among them." I wish that he had had that day a better, a more MIT-ish, MIT teacher.

That quiet afternoon in Dharamsala began a lifelong friendship. Among many cherished memories I particularly remember the time I arranged for him to speak at Syracuse. Someone in the audience asked him, "What should I do with my uncontrollable anger?" and the Dalai Lama sang out in

A mistake turns into a lifelong friendship. When I met the Dalai Lama in 1964 in Dharamsala, he assumed that, since I taught at MIT, I could answer all his pressing questions about science. Venerated in Tibet as practically a god, the Dalai Lama shows me rather what a fully developed human being can be. (Here, together at UCLA in 1991.)

English, "Control it." Another questioner kept goading him to assert Buddhism's superiority over Christianity. The Dalai Lama finally stopped the pest: "If I say anything against the Lord Jesus, the Buddha will scold me." Later, in Bodh Gaya, my student Phil Novak (later my coauthor of *Buddhism: A Concise Introduction*) asked the Dalai Lama to explain how rebirth works. Phil knew the usual metaphors of one candle flame lit from another or the apple seed that grows into a new apple tree, but he was still perplexed, saying, "We're not candles or trees, we're human beings." After reflecting a moment, the Dalai Lama answered, "Yes, something that might be called a self does continue from lifetime to lifetime, but it is so different from what we usually mean by *self* that it is better not to speak of it."

As I listened, I was reminded of the story of the man who asked the Buddha, "Is there no self?" When the Buddha gave no answer, the man exclaimed, "So there is a self!" to which again the Buddha made no reply. Later the Buddha's attendant asked him, "You always say there is no self. Why did you not answer the man?" The Buddha explained that the man had not wanted to heal himself or to help anyone but merely to form a theory. Helping and healing—not hypothesis and beliefs—were the Buddha's concerns as they have been the Dalai Lama's. Listening to him in Bodh Gaya, I felt I was not only at the place of the Buddha, but almost in his presence as well.

Back then my academic colleagues considered my interest in Buddhism odd and obsolete, as if I'd taken up, say, blacksmithing. Today every other person I know is, if not a Buddhist himself, someone whose sister or first cousin is. Why has Buddhism become so popular in America? The short answer: because it appeals to one's own experience, not dogma, and because it offers practical help. I used to wonder why Buddhism had no key poetic text the way Hinduism has the Bhagavad Gita and Taoism the Tao Te Ching. Then I realized that Buddhism deals less in poetic metaphors than in practical methods. And the starting point of those methods (as well as their end point) is your own mind.

Meditation is Buddhism's way of introducing you to your own mind. My good friend Heng Sure, a modern Buddhist hero, decided to go on a silent meditation walk, and the walk lasted three years. Heng Sure (an American who assumed

Out for a stroll. My friends Heng Sure and Heng Ch'au walked from Los Angeles to Ukiah, which, since they prostrated after every third step, took them three years. They showed that the epic feats of ancient Buddhist pilgrims in Asia could be done in the America of today.

a Chinese Buddhist name) undertook a pilgrimage on foot without speaking, walking from Los Angeles to Ukiah in northern California. It required three years because he did it in the traditional manner, taking three steps then bowing, taking three more steps then bowing, on and on, inching into the near and far. He thus inched through the Watts ghetto, where menacing youth shouted at him, "Look at the crazy honky!" and past the mansions of Beverly Hills, whose owners told him to grow up and get a job. With his vow of silence, he could not respond; he could only observe his reactions through the double mirror of his own and others' eyes.

Recently I asked Heng Sure what he learned from those three years. "Not much," he answered. "Perhaps just this: When I feel some urge, it does not push me immediately into action. I experience an extra split second of inner distance, and in that spilt second I can decide whether to act or not." Heng Sure's answer was modest, but isn't that the definition of freedom? We are free when we are not the slave of our impulses, but rather their master. Taking inward distance, we thus become the authors of our own dramas rather than characters in them.

When I think of freedom, or of the mind and its power, I think of the Dalai Lama at the precise moment he left Tibet. Behind him were the mountains of his homeland and everything he knew, now forever closed to him; before him lay the unknown horizon, where everything would be unaccustomed and unfamiliar. In his perilous escape he could bring with him nothing but his thoughts; he had nothing to offer the unknown world except his thoughts. Thoughts are intangible, ephemeral—as delicate as the flower the Buddha held out to his disciple. Yet from that flower, or rather from the Dalai Lama's thoughts, almost inconceivably, has arisen a whole new world of Buddhism in the West. As Daisetsu Suzuki said to me, "Is that fragile?"

III. ISLAM

I had sought out Hinduism and Buddhism, but it felt like Islam came in search of me. Of course I had taught it in my college courses, and I admired Muhammad as a great religious reformer who, among other achievements, improved the status of women in his time. The Holy Qur'an (or Koran) is, however, a difficult book for non-Muslims. I remember first reading it on a family vacation just as we were passing the Great Salt Lake in Utah. If you dove into the lake, its heavy salt content would practically bounce you back out of it. So, too, my attempts that summer to dive into the Holy

Qur'an were rebuffed. Little did I suspect then that I would embark on a decade-long, deeply personal involvement with Islam. It came about in this way.

In 1974 I was preparing to lead a group of students on a study year abroad. As soon as I arrived in Japan, I was to lecture on Shintoism, and, a drawback, I knew nothing about Shintoism. I noticed an unread book on my shelf, *On the Trail of Buddhism,* and—I can't resist peeking into any book—lo and behold, it had a chapter on Buddhism's ally in Japan, Shintoism. To boast, in Japan I gave a brilliant lecture on Shintoism. I simply parroted what the book's author, someone named Frithjof Schuon, had said. Later in India I chanced upon another volume by this Schuon called *Language of the Self,* which I thought equally brilliant. Still later I found Schuon's *Understanding Islam* to be the best introduction to the subject and his *Transcendent Unity of Religions* one of the best spiritual books I ever read. Wherever I ventured in the world's religions, Frithjof Schuon had been there before me. Who was he? I must meet him, I decided, if he is alive, whoever he is, wherever he might be.

He was indeed alive, and I tracked him down in Switzerland. When I met him there, he looked every inch a figure of mystery and romance. He wore flowing robes, and upon entering his presence, you kissed the ring on his finger. That is, if you could gain access to his presence, for he would not talk to just anyone. I had to first pass an interview with an attendant—the keeper of the gates, as it were—who had to approve of my position on matters important to Schuon. Did I, the attendant asked, believe in evolution? I sensed that if you accepted evolution, and not Majestic Divinity, as the key to explaining life, you would be bidden a polite adieu. In fact I do believe in evolution: the fossil record is a wondrous three-and-a-half-million-year story of man in the making. But on the technicality that evolutionary theory has not yet adequately explained consciousness, I answered a resounding, "Me? Evolution? Absolutely not!" I was then ushered into my audience with Frithjof Schuon.

The Romantic poets (Shelley, even Yeats) had fantasized about a fraternity of hidden adepts who practiced in secret throughout the world. Schuon headed such a secret order of Sufi adepts, and I had dreamed of belonging to something like it, before I even knew it existed. At our first meeting Schuon inquired what my own religious order was. When I answered Protestant, he shook his finger at me, pronouncing, "No. Christianity knows only two legitimate traditions, the Roman Catholic and the Eastern Orthodox." (Later, I was told, because of me Schuon came to accept Protestantism as a valid tradition as well.) The world overflows with glorious expressions of spirituality, he explained; but if you wanted to be in his fraternity, his *tariqa,* he urged you to become a Muslim.

Nothing on earth is easier than to become a Muslim. Want to inscribe yourself among the faithful? Then do as Schuon had me do and as millions of others have done: simply make a declaration of intent and swear belief in Allah (God). Schuon gave me my new initiate's name. I gasped. The Arabic syllables as they rolled off the tongue sounded so sonorous, charged with mystery, and as for their actual meaning—what insight Schuon had: of all possible names it was the name that I would have chosen for myself. What is it? In Schuon's *tariqa* one must not reveal his initiate name to outsiders, but upon hearing it, I knew a great adventure had begun.

A modern magus. Wherever I went exploring the world's religion, I often found Frithjof Schuon had been there before me. Schuon opened the door of Islam for me.

Frithjof Schuon opened the doors of Islam for me. I had been searching in the wrong places and looking in the wrong way. I thought Muhammad was a kind of avatar, somewhat like Jesus or the Buddha, but he is not that kind of incarnation. In fact Islam does have an "avatar": the Qur'an itself. But I had been reading the Qur'an in the wrong way. Admittedly it is not a book one curls up in bed with. Schuon unlocked the Qur'an by explaining that, while the Bible is history with theology thrown in, the Qur'an is theology ornamented with arabesques of history. The Bible moves you through historical time; the Qur'an intrudes you into the atemporal terrain of canonical truth. Once I absorbed that fact, the Qur'an spoke to me more poetically than poetry. In the Qur'an, God or Allah—referring to himself as "We"— talks directly and intimately to you. Muslims cannot understand how Christians can prize a book in which God is so inaccessible, talked about only in the third person.

To understand how Muslims communicate with God has grown my perspective, has enlarged my sense of the sacred. To learn what the Sufis mean by reality has made my own reality richer. Sufis, the mystics of Islam, do not want to hear about God at gossipy second hand. Most mystics don't want to read religious wisdom; they want to be it. A postcard of a beautiful lake is not a beautiful lake, and Sufis may be defined as those who dance in the lake. What drew me to the Sufis was in fact their dancing, how they pray not merely with their minds but with their bodies. I made a pilgrimage to Konya, where the poet Rumi and his fellow Sufis had whirled their bodies into prayers to God. And later I learned to dance that way myself.

In Tehran, an Iranian professor whom I had known in Boston arranged for me to attend a *majlis,* a Sufi gathering. The *majlis* took place not in a temple or shrine but in the basement of a house in an alley. Through a nondescript door I descended a narrow staircase into a dark, secretive world. Sufis have needed to exercise caution and shroud their activities from public view. They (and mystics in Christianity, too) have at times courted martyrdom by making their identity with the Divine too explicit. Thus the mystical Al-Hallaj wrote:

I saw my Lord with the eye of the heart. I said: "Who are you?"
He answered: "You."

In that basement *majlis* the dancing whirled till "I" and
"you" blurred in dizzying embrace.

Forty of us arranged ourselves in the basement in concentric circles. A faint light seeped through the transom, leaving
us shadowy silhouettes in the haunted dimness. Chanting began, which gradually turned to wailing. One by one we rose
to our feet, half hypnotized by the wail-like chanting, which
seemed to come from a collective voice at once ours and not
ours. Sometimes each danced in his own sphere, shuffling
from foot to foot. Then, unpremeditated, we would be holding hands, at other times locking arms around one another's
shoulders, as the tempo speeded up, as the pace became ever
more frenzied. Individual identities, self-consciousnesses, fell
away into whirling together in a semitrance. Of the forty men
there only I, trained to be the intellectual observer, was not
to pass over into a bliss beyond knowing. Surrounded by ec-
statics, I hovered between two worlds, on the shoreline, while
every face I looked at was in a transport of ecstasy. Rumi,
when dancing, was called to prayer, and he answered, "I am
already praying." So, too, the whirling men in that basement:
they dizzied and spun themselves into a sense of the divine.
After how long I cannot say, the wailing began to subside;
the whirling circles fragmented back into individual bodies. The men regrouped into two lines facing each other. Silently a scroll of white paper was unfurled between them, and
on it generous portions of couscous topped with raisins were
dished out. Those who had to work the next day departed after they finished their meal, but the old men lingered un-

til dawn, and I lingered with them, to bathe in the lingering glow of the *majlis*.

Ecstasy is only one mood and Sufism only one mode of Islam, and neither exhausted its appeal for me. Islam is a true path, coherent and communal and supportive, in a world that is too often none of these. The five pillars of Islam—from the affirmation of faith to the daily prayers, from Ramadan to the giving of alms—were pillars that supported and gave structure to my life for ten years. I never undertook the *hajj*, or pilgrimage to Mecca, which in any case is optional, depending on one's finances and health. I did observe Ramadan, fasting from sunup to sundown, eating in the middle of the night, until, out of sync with Kendra and the girls, it caused too much havoc in my household. I reluctantly excused myself from fasting during Ramadan on the authority of the Prophet, who declared that married life is half of holiness. Otherwise I was to be counted, by both conduct and inclination, among the faithful.

I especially valued the call to prayer five times a day, which I answered—I was going to say "religiously"—every day for twenty years. Praying at regular intervals imposed rhythm and structure on my activities, which can otherwise become diffuse and scatter in all directions. Jesus said to pray ceaselessly, but to pray all the time you probably need to be a saint, preferably one with a trust fund. In the Qur'an, Muhammad records a humorous dream in which he is the negotiator between Moses and God as they barter over how often one must pray. God at first says fifty times a day; Moses tells Muhammad to negotiate a lower figure. God reduces it to forty times, then twenty, then ten, and Moses still objects. When Muhammad finally gets it down to five times a day, he tells Moses: accept it, or you go talk to Him. Five times a day may be perfect. Those moments become like holy beads upon which consciousness through time, from our first arising to our at last lying down to sleep, is threaded. Osteoporosis today prevents me from performing the prostrations, but prayers in Arabic I can still do.

In the Qur'an, Allah is merciful, but he is also "ruler of the Day of Judgment." His goodness tempers his power, but his power compels our goodness, so that we don't behave like the spoiled child of an overly indulgent parent. My friend Virginia Gray Henry told me a funny story in which her merely referring to Allah's judgment dissolved all obstacles. Gray had been married to an Egyptian and lived for thirty years in Cairo, to which she returned after years away. Her taxi driver from the airport charged her an astronomical fare, which, with her knowledge of the city, she knew was exorbitant, but he would not back down. "All right," Gray said in impeccable Arabic, "I see you are stubborn and the hour is late and I am tired, so I will pay that amount. But remember this night, for on the Day of Judgment Allah will remember it." Hearing the invocation of Allah and the Day of Judgment, the cab driver broke down, begged her forgiveness, and refused to take any money at all.

On my bookshelf sits an old translation of the Qur'an by a Victorian convert to Islam, the delightfully named Marmaduke Pickthall. Traveling from gray England to the sunny Mideast, Pickthall became lighthearted, and he met, he said, for the first time truly happy people. Islam was for Pickthall—as it is to me—a mecca of order, meaning, beauty, and understanding. Today, however, when my countrymen look to the Middle East (especially since 9/11), they often look with eyes of fear and foreboding. In the West today no religion is more misunderstood than Islam; on both sides religion has gotten hijacked by politics. When I think how the Islam I saw by the light of spirituality is now obscured by the dark of ideology, my heart becomes heavy indeed.

I am at the end of my professional career, giving only an occasional talk. I won't be teaching any more students at MIT or Syracuse or Berkeley about Islam. Yet for one last time let me be the teacher and teach one last thing—a verse from the Qur'an: "If We [Allah is speaking] wished, We could have made you one people, but as it is, We have made you many. It is better this way. Therefore, vie among yourselves in good works." Elsewhere the Prophet tells us that in Paradise upon arrival all you do is say one word, over and over: *Peace—peace—peace.*

Peace.

7

THREE FINAL FRONTIERS

EARLIER I BOASTED THAT I CROSSED A DOZEN FRONTIERS IN my lifetime, the first of which was when I came to America and then embraced the life of the mind. Later frontiers of my life included mysticism, social involvement, and the world's religions; I moved into new territory when I became a writer and public person. However, if you are keeping a tally, you will notice that so far in this book I've named nine frontiers. Let me change the metaphor: instead of frontiers there were three more rungs which I had to ascend. The Middle Ages saw existence as a Great Chain of Being, a hierarchical ladder that climbed from the meagerest kind of limited life rung-by-rung up to *ens perfectissimum,* perfect being. *Ens perfectissimum* is not to be equated with enlightenment in the Asian sense, and yet thinking of it made me yearn for more.

I was to try three more rungs, to cross three more frontiers. First, though they had been under my nose the whole time, I discovered the Native American religions. My *Religions of Man* traced spirituality back only a few thousand years; with Native American and Australian Aboriginal friends I plunged into religions from the dawn mists of time. A second frontier of unexplored human possibilities opened up when Aldous Huxley and Timothy Leary introduced me to entheogens, psychedelic substances whose chemical assistance we hoped would allow us the mystical vision. I am not sure what to call the final rung of the ladder. I had become convinced that human beings are capable of a *knowing* not limited by our five senses. Plato said that most of us live in a dimly lit cave amid shadowy derivative reflections, but that it is possible to exit the cave and see what-is in clear light. That—a clear, unmitigated vision of things; ultimate reality—was my final frontier. I'll introduce these last frontiers in a paragraph each, and then we can cross over and explore them more fully.

I. Primal religions

When I moved to Syracuse in 1973, I assumed I was merely going from one university to another. Instead, that move propelled me into a different reckoning of our place in the universe, and all it took to radically change my understanding was a drive of five miles. I discovered that Syracuse was situated quite near the Onondaga Reservation. I soon took to spending my Saturdays on the reservation, schmoozing and drinking coffee with the chiefs. Returning home one Saturday, I exclaimed to myself in the car: "Huston! For thirty-five years you have circled the globe chasing distant gods, and here right before your eyes is a major religion you've failed to see." For all their seeming exoticism, earlier modes of spirituality have left psychic traces in our unconscious outlook. With that realization I proceeded to revise *The Religions of Man,* to bring the story around to where it began. (The revised edition, retitled *The World's Religions,* appeared in 1991.) Now at least I shall not go to my grave having authored a book on world religions that ignored the primal cauldron out of which they all arose.

Masai tribesmen. My encounters with "primal people" (so called) were always happy, but the Masai actually saved my life. When I got stranded in the Serengeti, they carried me *and* my broken-down car to the nearest habitation. From here, I told them, I can walk to the nearest town. If you do, they warned, you *must* be eaten by lions.

II. Entheogens

William James observed, after taking nitrous oxide, that our normal waking consciousness "is but one special type of consciousness" and that "there lie potential forms of consciousness entirely different. [Simply] apply the requisite stimulus." I applied the requisite stimulus. Since the word *psychedelics* evokes the "tune in, turn on, drop out" mind-set of the 1960s, I prefer the word *entheogens* (meaning "God enabling") for nonaddictive substances that are used to explore the hidden dimensions of the mind James was referring to. When I took consciousness-altering entheogens, research on them was not only legal but respectable. Aldous Huxley described mescaline as the most "significant experience available to human beings this side of the Beatific Vision." What ten years on a

Zen meditation cushion had failed to bring about—*satori*—came about on January 1, 1961, an hour after I swallowed two doses of it.

III. *"Ultimate reality"*

I had my first taste of something unqualified and luminous that morning I told you about in chapter 1, when I was five or six, and I felt the dew between my toes and watched the dawn mists parting to reveal a sunny clarity and freshness everywhere. The curtains again seemed to part that New Year's Day I took mescaline with Tim Leary. Methods are many—monks meditate; Sufis dance; penitents fast—to obtain a larger, sacred sense of existence. One of my methods was being married to Kendra. Have a wife who is somewhat psychic, and reality, or our knowledge of it, will grow porous, mysterious, and friendly. Once in Death Valley I had a sense of crossing *into* the landscape and becoming part of reality from the other side. If human life is to survive on this planet, the old dualistic worldview, with people on one side and the environment on the other, must yield to a new vision that connects us with everything else and leads us to care for and take responsibility for it.

Primal religions, entheogens, and confronting "ultimate reality" (through psychic experiences or otherwise)—each teach us this lesson of interconnectedness in its own way. Native American religions see the solitary individual and the communal whole as two sides of the same coin. Psychic experiences view subject and object—"I" and "it"—as the inside and outside of the same fabric. Psychoactive drugs also can cause the wall separating inner and outer to crumble. William Blake said that each person must free himself from prison— the prison of being a limited, corporeal, dying self. Primal religions, entheogens, and an enhanced sense of reality are each keys for unlocking the prison door.

PRIMAL RELIGIONS

Dzang Zok, China, may have been the other side of the world, but that didn't stop me when I was a boy from imagining I was an American Indian. In the forest primeval—that is to say, among the tomato vines in our backyard—my brothers and I played Indian braves, the arrows flying from our bows, for we were on the warpath. At the Shanghai American School we performed Longfellow's *Song of Hiawatha,* and its "By the shores of Gitche Gumee, / by the shining Big-Sea-Water" rhymed a wild native America into my imagination. My first brush with the Native American legacy, caricature thought it was, would come to fruition a half century later on those Saturdays on the Onondaga Reservation.

What a lovely way to spend part of the weekend. The Onondaga chiefs and I became easy with each other. I felt comfortable enough to reproach Chief Oren Lyons, a particularly good friend, with something that bothered me: "Oren, you are a bunch of male chauvinists. Why aren't any of your chiefs women?" Oren was gentle with my ignorance: "Huston, all our chiefs are appointed by the women." (Charlotte Black Elk later told me that her tribe, the Oglala Sioux, even have a separate spiritual language, Hambloglagia, taught only to and spoken only by women.) OK about the women, I thought, but then I saw what was labeled a "Six Nations Passport" lying on the table. By now I knew that the Onondagas were one of the original nations of the Iroquois Confederacy—the oldest living democracy on the continent—but *really*. "Really, Oren," I said, pointing to the passport, "I thought you'd be above such tourist gimmicks." Oren explained that, overcoming many an obstacle, with that very passport he had traveled to Geneva, to a conference of indigenous peoples. I was impressed: here was not a bygone way of life but one that, defying oppression and extinction, is using its wiles and remaining vital in the present.

When the Onondagas and other Iroquois held their annual meeting, Oren invited me to stop by and meet the visiting chiefs. A fine morning it was, full of goodwill, with stories swapped back and forth. Then Oren looked at his watch. "It's eleven," he said. "Time to begin." He said to me, "We are going into the longhouse, but you cannot. Huston, we know you're on our side, but an outsider's presence would profane it." Instead of feeling insulted, I was elated. Hooray!—there are still truths too precious to broadcast to just any and everyone. I asked Oren how long the meeting would last, thinking I might wait outside, but he could not tell me. Their "bible," *The Legend of Handsome Lake,* has never been committed to writing because it's considered a living entity. At the annual meeting the chiefs recite it, and if there's any disagreement, they discuss and discuss it, however long is necessary, until consensus is reached. Once long ago Hindus and Buddhists and the Greeks had so passed on their myths and truths, but even today the Onondagas return us to that time, preserving their sacred vision orally from generation to generation. I felt it an honor to be excluded.

Oren Lyons, a great Onondaga chief and wisdom keeper. Mircea Eliade argued that "primitive" people are more spiritually advanced than their modern counterparts. After getting to know Oren Lyons, I repudiated the word *primitive* and acknowledged their spiritual sophistication.

Barred from the longhouse, I learned truths from the Onondagas anyway. I learned that an individual is not a solitary figure alone under the indifferent heavens. When Oren returned home during his college semester break—Oren was the first Onondaga to attend college—his uncle, he told me, invited him on a fishing trip. When they were in the middle of the lake his uncle said, "Oren, you've been to college. You must be pretty smart now. Let me ask: who are you?"

Oren: "What do you mean, Uncle? You know me. I'm your nephew."

His uncle simply said it again, "Who are you?"

"I'm Oren Lyons."

"No!"

"I am an Onondaga."

"No!"

"I'm a human being."

"No!"

When Oren had exhausted every conceivable answer, his uncle pointed to the shore: "Do you see that bluff over there? You *are* that bluff. And that giant pine on the other shore? Oren, you are that pine. And this water that supports our boat? You are this water." In place of a proud and defiant ego, his uncle had demoted and promoted Oren into being (of) the earth itself.

Oren's story made me think of the time my father commissioned the local silversmith to make a silver tea set, to impress visitors to Dzang Zok. Wanting it to be impressive— nay, perfect—he kept telling the poor man how to do his job. The man, who was following the family trade for generations, took offense: "Enough! I have been a silversmith for four hundred years."

We are like that silversmith, part of a large extended family. I learned that lesson from Douglas George, my only Native American student at Syracuse. The particular morning I am thinking of began at 6 a.m., when the phone's ringing roused me from my sleep. It was my younger brother, Walt, who blurted out that our older brother, Robert, had died, from a blood clot in his brain. Distracted, upset, I taught my ten o'clock class anyway, but I explained to them what had happened, in case I was unusually incoherent. I managed to get through it somehow. As I left the classroom, Douglas fell in step with me, and we walked silently back to my office. Once inside, Douglas said, "Professor Smith, I am sorry it happened. When something like this happens among our people [he is a Mohawk-Iroquois], we sit together." He sat with me in my office for twenty minutes, saying not another word. His silent company was the most comforting condolence and a lesson in how in sorrow not to be alone. Thinking of Douglas's kindness, I asked Oren Lyons what it meant to him to be an Indian. He answered matter-of-factly, "It means to help others."

The Onondagas were not, however, my first experience of a primal religion. In 1962, I was invited to give the first Charles Strong Lectures in World Religions at the major universities of Australia. The schedule was not demanding, and at each university my hosts would politely inquire how I wanted to spend my free time. My answer: "With your anthropology department. Learning about Aborigines." Every anthropologist I met believed that Aborigines had psychic powers. All the anthropologists told stories of, for example, some Aborigine abruptly ending a long trek because he intuited that some relative had died, and every time the premonition proved correct. Every anthropologist I talked with was convinced that telepathic ability is native to human beings, but we have lost it by relying on telegraphs and telephones and television. In Melbourne I met Jim Morgan, a citified Aborigine who could speak English. When he saw that my interest was sincere, he left his city clothes behind and led me into the bush. As we would fall asleep camping by a river he regaled me with stories his grandmother had told him, stories she had heard from her grandmother, who in turn had heard them from. . . . Under the starry skies I was falling asleep to the lullaby of eternity.

One anthropologist asked me how far north in Australia I was going. When I answered, "Perth," he said, "Pity." He showed me a *National Geographic* article he'd written about the Tiwis on Melville Island, an article that he hoped I might deliver there. I heard opportunity knocking: I booked a ticket to Darwin and from there hired a pilot for the short flight to the islands. I arranged to stay with the Australian in charge of the tiny government station there and was so exhausted I fell asleep at once on his couch. Suddenly I bolted awake to his yelling, "Get the hell out of here!" He was giving a kangaroo a swift kick in the backside.

The Tiwis had never seen a magazine before, nor, for that matter, a photograph. They looked at the *National Geographic* picture of one Tiwi boy and immediately burst into tears. The boy, it turned out, had since died. When they saw another boy's picture in the magazine, they clamped their palms over it. Not knowing what photos were, they thought they were looking at the boy's spirit. It lay there so visible and unprotected on the page that evil spirits could seize it, and they cupped their hands over the photo to protect him.

The Australian stationmaster told me that no white person could possibly understand the Tiwi worldview. The words they used did not mean what they seem to mean. Their "Dreaming" occurs when waking; their "Dreamtime" denies or defies time. For the Tiwis, yesterday and today and tomorrow are not an arrow that shoots from past to present to future; rather all tenses, and sleeping and waking, mix and cohabit in an atemporal duration beyond clocks and calendars. The aboriginal world began long ago when the Ancestors sang in Dreamtime the cosmic rhythms that give shape to the things we see, and it is beginning right now, when a living Tiwi sings the Dream songs that continue, or are, the world.

Since they never underwent the Neolithic revolution, in which hunter-gatherers became settled agriculturists, the

In Melbourne I met Jim Morgan, a citified Aborigine. When he found out my interest was genuine, he led me into the bush where I felt immersed in a time when the clock had stuck at eternity. (Jim had made the toy boomerang in my hand.)

Tiwis, like other Aborigines, remain the closest living people to the earth's original human inhabitants. Yet to understand their worldview, I had to consult the most scientifically advanced people alive today, quantum physicists. Ancient wisdom and postmodern science make unlikely bedfellows, and yet they often say, in quite different dialects, similar things. In quantum mechanics the observer determines (or even brings into being) what is observed, and so, too, for the Tiwis, who dissolve the distinction between themselves and the cosmos. In quantum physics, subatomic particles influence each other from a distance, and this tallies with the aboriginal view, in which people, animals, rocks, and trees all weave together in the same interwoven fabric. The Tiwis may be the most "primitive" society I ever encountered, but they were also the least alienated from their surroundings. They thus prepared me for Onondagas, for otherwise I might not have understood how people can be so at home in their world.

The Native Americans I later met felt themselves, like the Tiwis, kin to all living things on the planet. They were not blind to differences: indigenous peoples are famous for their powers of observation. The Onondagas saw distinctions as bridges, however, not as barriers. Addressing a United Nations meeting in 1977, Oren Lyons commented: "I do not see a delegation for the Four Footed. I see no seat for the Eagles. . . " Never had the United Nations had more nations in it.

Oren is an extraordinary chief and wisdom keeper, but any Onondaga youth might have expressed the same sentiments. For an international youth program in New York City, I arranged for a young Onondaga to preside at the opening ceremony. Under a large oak tree in Central Park he said, "Let us begin with a prayer." I bowed my head for the minute or so the prayer would take. After thirty minutes, the prayer (which was in the Onondaga language) showed no sign of ending. Opening my eyes, I noticed that our young leader's head was not bowed, nor were his eyes closed. His gaze kept turning in all four directions, looking up at the sky, then down at the ground. After the ceremony he explained to me, "I needed to call upon every living thing in the area—the trees, the birds, the stones, the clouds, and the earth itself—to invite their participation. Otherwise our gathering will lack sacredness."

Inspired by him and by Oren Lyons, my interest in Native-American causes took off. I coauthored with Reuben Snake *One Nation Under God.* Next, I helped get Congress to overturn the legal ban on peyote, which has been a Native Americans sacrament for a thousand years (and never once been associated with a single crime). I like how the Comanche chief Quanah Parker described the spiritual effects of peyote: "In their church white people talk *about* Jesus; in ours we talk *with* Jesus." I always felt happier at Native American gatherings than at meetings of the American Academy of Religion or, for that matter, at the universities where I taught for fifty years.

Why? I wonder. Perhaps it's because primal people see the objects of this world not (or not only) as solid but as open windows to their divine source. We moderns have severed the connection. But for Native Americans—as for the Tiwis—material things grow out of their spiritual roots, and appearance always has another side to it. As that Native American classic *Black Elk Speaks* puts it:

> It is often difficult for those who look on the tradition of the Red Man from the outside or through the "educated" mind to understand that no object is what it appears to be, but it is simply the pale shadow of a Reality. It is for this reason that every created object is *wakan,* holy, and has a power according to the loftiness of the spiritual reality it reflects.

When I spend time with Native Americans, I feel somewhat as I do when I travel in the other India. The poverty on the subcontinent is almost intolerable, and disease is (or was) rampant, yet I always found myself more lighthearted there. A sense of holiness is in the air, as it is with Native Americans, in a way not known on the streets of New York or San Francisco.

ULTIMATE REALITY (AS GLIMPSED THROUGH PSYCHIC EXPERIENCES)

The book *Black Elk Speaks* enthralled my generation. I had a chance to meet its author, John Niehardt, when I taught a semester at Stephens College in Columbia, Missouri, and he was the visiting professor of journalism at the University of Missouri. I prepared a hundred questions to ask him about Native American religion, and I got to ask—not one. Niehardt was too preoccupied with what had happened the day before. An insurance agent had come out to Niehardt's house to investigate his claim about a minor car accident. The agent was unaccountably on edge and finally said, "Would you mind putting that dog out? He's making me nervous." "What dog?" John asked. The agent said, "That little black spaniel," but then glanced under the table and added, "Oh, he seems to have gone out by himself." The Niehardts had indeed owned a black spaniel, dear to them as a child, but it had died the week before. That uncanny incident of the ghost dog was all John could talk about during my visit—or perhaps ever again. He lost all interest in completing his epic poem on the Midwest and instead founded the Center for the Study of Paranormal Phenomena.

Aborigines may be psychic, but insurance agents? Philosophers like myself fear losing their credibility if we discuss scientifically inexplicable things such as psychic abilities. Yet psychic experiences do serve a purpose: they challenge our conventional assumptions about both ourselves and the world. My assumptions get regularly challenged before I even leave my house—by having Kendra as my wife. Let me give you an example. Kendra was away taking a course, studying

Eileen Garrett. My friend Eileen Garrett was perhaps the most respected medium and psychic researcher of the twentieth century. Spending time with Eileen convinced Kendra and me that reality (or realities) contains more and subtler interconnections than most of us suspect.

the farfetched (to me) possibility of healing from a distance. Unbeknownst to me, she used me as her guinea pig, trying through mental effort from afar to cure the neuritis or eye ache from which I had been suffering for several months. By the time she returned, my neuritis was healed, but I chalked that up to coincidence. I pooh-poohed "psychic healing," but when I threw my back out while lifting a heavy box of books, I sheepishly asked her if she might, well, try something. Kendra appeared to go into some altered state, and who knows what she did—or even if that was the cause—but my back felt immediately better. Later that day I threw it out again, lifting another load of books, but when I requested psychic healing this time, Kendra refused: "You know, Huston, there are limits." She was right; it was my own fault. But challenging or changing limits is what psychic ability is about. It rearranges our understanding of reality, and in that new reality one should be able to be healed from self-inflicted back injury twice in the same day.

Personally I have no talent in the psychic area. In 1984, however, I witnessed the ultimate kind of psychic experience, one that changed my understanding of our relationship to "nature." Kendra and I were staying in Death Valley, the lowest geographic point in the United States. In the night she woke up and felt compelled to go outside. The desert, she later told me, seemed to be calling her; it somehow required her. She walked and walked until she lost awareness of herself in that vast and dark-lit space. She felt that nothing separated her from the desert; that they were one thing assuming different shapes. If I search for a metaphor for Kendra's experience, it was like wallpaper being slicked onto a wall: she was a tissue-thin sheet plastered onto an environment without end.

That night in Death Valley seemed to Kendra like "ultimate reality"; she was, it seemed, in a world beyond momentary appearances. My good friend Ann Jauregui says that such experiences are not rare, although most people forget or attach no importance to them. Ann told me about hers, when she was a young girl in Michigan. In summer she would lie on a wooden raft anchored in the bay, listening to the waters lapping, drowsy in the warm sunshine. The warm day, the clear northern light, and the water's gentle motion together worked a semihypnotic effect. Then suddenly Ann would snap alert and feel intensely alive, or rather that everything was alive and she was part of it. The rocks, the rowboats on the shore, the water itself—everything seemed pulsating with a kind of energy. She found she could put questions to the experience. "What is my role in all this?" she asked. "I want to

Death Valley. One night when Kendra and I were in Death Valley it felt as though she had crossed through the landscape and entered nature, as though from its other side.

know," she whispered. "Show me." The rock, the trees, the water—all in silent chorus "answered"—not in words, of course—that her wanting to know, just that, was her part of the pulsating landscape. "Creation delights in the recognition of itself" is how she would later put it. She never talked about her experiences then—it seemed important not to—but recently she described them in a book called *Epiphanies.* When she gives talks about her book, half the people in the audience will exclaim, "Yes! That happened to me, too."

Noam Chomsky was my colleague at MIT for fifteen years; he was one of the few geniuses I have met. I recall Chomsky saying that a cat cannot be expected to do algebra, so why should human beings with their cognitive limitations expect to fathom all the laws of the universe. I agree with Chomsky, except that for *limitations* I would substitute *mystery.* We are born in mystery, we live in mystery, and we die in mystery. The value of psychic experience is that it deepens the mystery, not that it dispels it.

I do not need to visit psychics: I have a wife at home. I taught the great religions, but Kendra lived them, or the empathetic interconnections they teach, effortlessly. Often she would come home from her work as a psychotherapist with some story like this one. A working-class client had that day kept voicing Kendra's thoughts, what was going on in her mind, before she could say it aloud. The man also told her, "You have a bad pain in your hip." He knew, he explained, because he had absorbed the pain and was now feeling it in *his* hip. But don't worry, he added, after he left he would pass it on to someone else. "No, you won't!" she exclaimed. "Sit back down." Living with Kendra was a reminder to this professor that there are other ways of knowing and other knowledges to know. The other day someone asked Kendra the secret of our long marriage. She answered, or avoided answering, "Oh, I cut items out of the newspaper to show Huston, and I think he likes that." It is not the secret, of course, but she does show me "items" from a subtler news—news from ultimate reality—and I do like that.

ENTHEOGENS

At a talk at Harvard the theologian Paul Tillich asked what he called the question of our century: "Is it possible to regain the lost dimension—the [direct] encounter with the Holy?" This was in the mid-twentieth century, when genuine religious experiences seemed to be drying up and religious rituals were turning rote and formulaic. Some seekers resorted to clairvoyants and mediums, and even to a preoccupation with flying saucers, to bolster their belief that there was something else out there. Aldous Huxley's *The Doors of Perception* (1954) excited me, precisely because it promised a larger reality. Huxley's experiences with mescaline suggested a new way, an untried door. (Later, learning about the Native American rite of peyote, I realized that chemically induced religious visions were as old as human history. The Eleusinian Mysteries, whose initiates included Plato and Pythagoras, employed such psychoactive potions.) I filed this new/old possibility away to follow up on someday—when or how I did not know.

The new decade of the 1960s (long before they became *the sixties!*) brought an interesting conjunction of two visitors to Boston. I arranged for Aldous Huxley to lecture at MIT, which led to our discussing in private his mescaline experiences. Seeing my interest, Aldous suggested I meet, a mile up the Charles River, a new researcher at Harvard University. The researcher was Timothy Leary, and it turned out he was eager to meet me. Having taken hallucinogenic mushrooms in Mexico the previous summer, Tim was now a man on a mission, and hallucinogens—specifically LSD—became his research subject at Harvard. Although little was known about it then, LSD inspired great hopes in sociomedical circles. Used therapeutically, could it keep paroled convicts from returning to old, destructive patterns? Might it help alcoholics break their alcoholic dependency? To answer such questions, Tim was conducting LSD experiments with volunteers. He was puzzled when they kept comparing the effects of the drug to a mystical experience. During our lunch at the Harvard Faculty Club, he asked me whether that

Aldous Huxley. Huxley, when I knew him, ranked as one of the giants of twentieth-century literature. His visionary experiences with mescaline led me to use entheogens to advance one rung—forgive the wordplay—*higher* on the Great Chain of Being.

comparison held any validity. Soon, however, our discussion shifted beyond academic theory. All right, when? We got out our pocket calendars to arrange a date to be guinea pigs ourselves—no, this date wouldn't work; not that one, either—and eventually settled on New Year's Day 1961.

Shortly after noon on that cold January 1, Kendra and I arrived at Tim's house in Newton. Laid out on the coffee table were the hors d'oeuvres: one capsule was a mild dose, Tim said; two, average; and three would make a walloping helping of mescaline. I took one, and Kendra, more venturesome, took two. Soon the world mutated into a bewitched carnival, significant and terrifying beyond belief. Space multiplied

Timothy Leary. Huxley said of Leary that he had never met a more handsome man, never a more charming man, but asked, Why does he have to be such an ass? Well, Tim was an Irish rebel and his perennial rebellion got him kicked out of everything from West Point to Switzerland. He encouraged the generation of the sixties to "tune in, turn on, and drop out." I began the Sixties—New Year's Day, 1961—by taking mescaline with him and for the next few hours experienced the mystical vision.

into not three or four dimensions but more like twelve. There were at least five bands or layers of mental activity going on, which I could move back and forth among at will. Lying on the living-room couch, I could hear Tim's conversation in the kitchen and participate in it imaginatively, even as I exited it to ascend into an ecstatic, unearthly light that made that conversation comically trivial. I watched the clear, unbroken light as it fractured and condensed into things around me. I nearly laughed aloud: if the ancient Indian *rishi*s and mystical philosophers like Plotinus had had experiences like mine— and probably they had—they were not speculative geniuses; they were hack reporters.

Supposedly no person can look directly into the face of God and live. (It would be like plugging your electric shaver into a power line.) After a dozen or so hours I felt that my animal nature had ascended step-by-step up to the very borderland of divinity. There remained only the final all-consuming stage of limitless bliss, but if I dared cross over into it, my body, I felt, might explode or implode from the electric overload of ecstasy. I called to Tim in the kitchen, "Do you know what you're playing around with? You could have a corpse on your couch." No sooner did I say *corpse* than my body felt cool and moist, as though laid out on an undertaker's slab. All the effort I could muster went into willing myself to stay in my body. Slowly the bliss began to evaporate, and the objects around me resumed their familiar shape. Everything (including me) put back on its mask of normality, albeit slightly askew, as I got up from the couch. Centuries had passed, it seemed, since we had arrived at Tim's house, when Kendra and I got into the car and drove home through the cold January night. We found our children asleep in their beds, sleeping the sleep of the innocent, and never in my life did Karen and Gael and Kim look more precious to me than they did then.

So, the big question: what was January 2 like? Overnight I had become a visionary, someone who not only believes in a larger world but has actually visited it. What the mystics had sung were not poetic metaphors but real experiences, I knew now. The Sufis say there are three ways to know fire— by hearing it described, by seeing it, or by being burned. I was, in that analogy, now burned by the fire. But one must not be consumed but bring the fire—or whatever name we give our experience of ultimate reality—back home, to warm our hands and live by.

The questions people ask me about mescaline (apart from "Where can I get some?") are: "How often did you take it?" and "How did drugs change you?" Easy to answer. After a few trials, I ate no more mescaline hors d'oeuvres, small, medium, or large. As Ram Dass told me, "After you get the message, hang up." Nor did they radically change my thinking, for I already subscribed to the worldview of the mystics. Thanks to entheogens, though, I experienced what I had previously believed. Entheogens are not to be lightly trifled with: more than once a phone call from Niagara Falls woke me during the night: the person had taken LSD, panicked, and was considering jumping into the falls. However, if taken with the right attitude and in the proper setting, psychoactive drugs may produce religious experiences. Let me, however, print a further warning label on the bottle: it is far less clear that they can produce religious lives. A religion made up solely of heightened religious experiences would not be a religion at all. After his great awakening, the Buddha continued to meditate and to devote himself to others; otherwise his vision would have receded into a pleasant memory. The major religious traditions address the mysteries (with or without entheogens), but they have other business to do: widen understanding, give meaning, provide solace, promote loving-kindness, and connect human being to human being.

This is my litmus test for entheogens, or indeed for any mental experience however induced: does it enhance your whole life, and then do you in turn enhance the lives of others? Aldous Huxley was asked how his taking mescaline affected him, and I was amused by his answer. "I may be-come a slightly better person," he said. "For a few days." From entheogens, and from my encounter with Native American religion, and from my glimpses of "ultimate reality"—and from the nine other frontiers I crossed—I may have become a slightly better person, and, I pray, for longer than a few days.

EPILOGUE

Reflections upon Turning Ninety

May 31, 2009. Ninety years old. As my birthday nears, people are congratulating me as though I'd done something—run a marathon blindfolded, say. That may not be an entirely inaccurate description of reaching ninety, but never before have I been congratulated for doing nothing, or nothing more than continuing to breathe in and out. Behind the congratulations, though, I sometimes detect fears and a need for reassurance that it will be all right. The fears are real. And all will be all right.

A year ago, however, I did do something. I moved from my home on Colusa Avenue, full of air and light and with my study overlooking Berkeley's golden hills, and moved into one room in an assisted-living facility. I left Kendra, my intimate companion of sixty-five years, to cohabit with people in wheelchairs or depressed or with Alzheimer's. "I had already been in assisted living for half a decade," I joke and point to Kendra. "She was the assister." (My increasing physical needs were taking their toll on her health; hence the move.) The first night after the move was a dark night of the soul. Religion relies on that successful plot device, the happy ending. I still believed in one, but after my first night in the assisted-living

A friend whom I am like. The folksinger Pete
Seeger and I were born in the same month, on
the same day, in the same year. We resemble
each other physically, too, and Pete is also going
strong at ninety. When he was blacklisted during
the McCarthy era, I invited him to perform and
stay with us whenever possible. My children
relished his visits, for he would turn any conceivable (and inconceivable) object, like a garbage-
can lid, into a musical instrument.

residence I thought, The happy ending will now have to wait
until I am dead.

And then after three days here, it became acceptable, per-
fectly fine. The move seemed no more than turning the page
of a book. On the previous page I had been on Colusa Avenue and on this page I am here, but the story itself has not
changed. And ninety, I discover, is a good age for making
new friends. The maintenance man, Mr. Lin, has just left my

A friend whom I am not like. The mythologist
Joseph Campbell downgraded religion to the
status of "myth" because it had so marred his
childhood in Scotland. Religion to me, even
in childhood, has always embodied reality (or
realities), whose presence and wonder I experience daily.

room, and how coincidental: he grew up in China near where
I grew up! We have wonderful conversations, in Chinese. Today Mr. Lin told me how during the Cultural Revolution
(when Mao boasted he had eradicated hunger) there was no
leaf on any tree; people plucked and ate them, to stave off
starvation. "Mr. Lin," I asked, "did you eat the leaves, too?"
"Ah, Huston, I believe I am alive, am I not? Yes, I ate the
leaves, too."

People go to nursing homes, I've heard it said, to die. I came to this assisted-living residence, it seems, to cheer people up. I still begin each day with exercise for the body, reading religious classics for my mind, and prayer for the spirit. I have modified the physical exercises, since I can no longer stand on my head (although if my osteoporosis bends me over much more I won't be far from it). Now to the threefold body-mind-spirit morning regimen, I have added a fourth practice. Mentally I take a census of the other residents here, and as each appears in my imagination, I ask how I might improve his or her day.

The other residents are dear, but often their conditions are not. In the dining room the conversation can be minimal, except for one incessant chatterbox everyone ignores. I will use any topic to get the ball rolling: "Mr. Lin told me today that in Chinese astrology this is the year of the rat." The others at the table ask what that means, and soon everyone is free-associating about rats, and we're on our way. We're always on our way, if only we knew it. A former surgeon here has trouble hearing, and I offered to introduce him to a famous hearing expert I know. "No, no, Huston," he answered, "thanks, but I'm fine." I do not understand that attitude. Oliver Sacks says that deafness cuts you off from society even more than blindness. I had a risky cochlear-implant operation to improve my hearing: I want to hear what everyone says, even the chatterbox. It has meaning, and it may help me figure things out.

At our "Spiritual Moments" meeting, Father James gets us going using a deck of cards with a word written on each one, and when he extracts one, we each say our associations with that particular word. When the word was *beauty,* I immediately thought: *Kendra!* This week Father James was absent, so I took his place: in pantomime I drew from an imaginary deck an imaginary card and said the word *gratitude*. Gratitude—what I learned from the *roshi* at the Kyoto monastery half a lifetime ago. I could obsess about my ailments and be an old man in misery. Instead I forget them and wonder how I came to be so fortunate and what I am even doing in an assisted-living home. Gratitude? If I fail to mention something in a letter but remember before I put it in the mailbox, I feel grateful. The day sings its song of small grace notes. In the bathroom or the elevator I whisper under my breath, "God, you are so good to me"—thirty-five or forty times a day I say it. It seems I finally have a mantra.

✿ ✿ ✿

"God, you are so good to me." After a lifetime of studying and teaching and writing, of investigating, deliberating, and philosophizing, of heaping qualification upon qualification, how simple it can finally become.

People ask me questions like "Do you still practice Hinduism?" Or "What role does Buddhism play in your life today?" Dare I answer? I have forgotten more about the various religions than I knew in the first place. All that is left of my study of them is…me.

My father had black-and-white ideas, a right and a wrong way for every situation. When Kendra and I were first married, I watched her spread jam on her toast, and I repeated my father's stricture: "The first piece of toast, no jam. On the second piece jam is permissible." "But I am eating only one piece," Kendra replied. "Oh," I thought, perplexed, "well…in that case I guess it's all right." Six and a half decades of living with Kendra has gotten me over arbitrary notions and helped bring me into the open air of simply being.

Religion teaches us that our lives here on earth are to be used for transformation. Buddhism in particular describes three mental toxins by which we poison ourselves—greed, hatred and delusion—but it is possible to transform those poisons into three blessings. Kendra would readily admit that her "poison" is hatred, but hatred, when purified, turns into discernment, and Kendra has become the most discerning person I know. (When I was a judge for the Danforth fellowships, I'd turn the applications over to her; she had some magical sixth sense for who the right applicants were.) Care to guess my poison? Me, who wanted to be a big man on campus at Central College, who hungered always for more experience, who enjoyed what small bits of acclaim came his way? Yet Buddhism says that greed, purified, becomes great faith. As I enter my tenth decade on earth, my faith does seem to be enlarging, not in opposition to experience but coming out of it.

"At age thirty"—this is the sage Confucius speaking—"I could stand on my own feet. At age forty I suffered no more doubts. At fifty I understood the mandate of heaven. But only at age sixty could I do what I wanted without going against the path." Possibly I needed to go through ninety years of life to understand how life itself is the path.

And one day the path shall end. I am thinking now of my beautiful daughter Karen and her premature death. After her death an interviewer asked me—I still hear his question— "Can you believe in God's perfection now?" No, when Karen

In 1996 Bill Moyers did a five-part TV special, *The Wisdom of Faith with Huston Smith*. Those interviews were like intimate conversations about the world's religions with a close friend, upon which public television happened to be eavesdropping.

lay dying, I could no longer see any justice or perfection. Or perhaps I did feel it, through my tears, in the heroic way our daughter met her end. On her last day, after the sarcoma cancer (I described it earlier) had spread into all her organs, causing excruciating pain, she told me, "I have no complaints" and "I am at peace." Her last words were about the sea, which symbolized life to her: how she could even smell it, it was so near. Her death, so unbittered and brave, increases, if not my sense of perfection, my awe. Only Karen or someone upon whom the worst has fallen has the right to absolve life of our possible grievances against it. The father learned nobility of spirit from the daughter.

※ ※ ※

Socrates called philosophy the practice of dying. I have puzzled over that statement, unsure of what Socrates meant. In the *Phaedo* he said death will be either a restful sleep or a meeting of noble souls in a better world, and hence why fear? With Karen's example before me, I believe death holds no terror for me. Perhaps I have practiced philosophy in the way Socrates intended after all.

How would I like to die? My friend Martin Lings, author of *Return to the Spirit,* wrote his last book when older than I am now. An avid gardener, Martin went into his garden and picked a bloom of uncommon beauty and put it in a vase. And with no more fuss he slumped over, *adieu.* People tell you, however, that you cannot choose how or when you will die. In fact I have known two people who did choose. The abbot of a monastery in Kyoto, upon retirement, retreated into a tiny hut, where one day he summoned the monks and announced he planned to die that coming Friday. "You cannot!" they exclaimed. "Friday begins O Bon!" O Bon is that busy time when the monastery's patrons and parishioners visit; his death would get in the way. Obliging, my friend postponed his dying to the next month. I cannot hope to emulate him, but nonetheless I take a lesson from his example. The lesson: our common fears and assumptions about death may be just that—assumptions—that have little to do with the reality.

People ask me, the professor of religion, "What happens when we die?" Every time, I think of the student who approached the Zen master.

STUDENT: What happens when we die?
ZEN MASTER: I don't know.
STUDENT: But you're a Zen master!
ZEN MASTER: True. Quite true. But I am not a dead Zen master.

I am not a dead religion professor—yet. However, most of us do have unexamined or unconscious assumptions about what happens after we shed this mortal coil. Although none of our surmises can be proved, there may be a reason or resonance why we each imagine what we do. So pull up a chair, have a seat, and I'll tell you (my idea of) what happens when we die.

Charles Tart, in the psychology department at the University of California at Davis, has devoted his career to studying clairvoyance, telepathy, psychokinesis, and out-of-body experiences. I asked him if he thought his consciousness would survive his bodily death. "Yes, definitely," Charles answered, only he did not know whether *he* (or it) would still recognize it as *his* consciousness. Charles's answer raises a question. If we survive beyond this single lifespan, do we (a) survive as individuals, or (b) dissolve into something greater ("the Godhead")? Sri Ramakrishna opted or hoped for the first possibility: "I want to taste sugar. I don't want to be sugar." In *Why Religion Matters* I expressed my intuition: we are each allowed to choose for ourselves the possibility we want.

I give myself poetic license to imagine it. After I shed my body, I will remain conscious of old habits and habitations;

I will still be concerned with Kendra, Gael, Kim, and the whole *dramatis personae* of my life on earth. However, a day will come when no one alive will have heard of Huston Smith, much less have known him. What will be the point of my hanging around then? I will turn my back on this dear world and direct my attention to something more interesting: the beatific vision. So long as I remain involved with my individuality, I'll be aware that it is Huston Smith enjoying this vision. For me, though—mystic that I am at heart—after oscillating back and forth between enjoying the sunset and enjoying Huston-Smith-enjoying-the-sunset, I expect that the uncompromised sunset will become ever more absorbing. The branch of narrowed awareness upon which I rested will sever and fall away. The bird will be set free.

Soon it will be time to say good-bye. Let me end where I began, by saying good-bye first to you, my mother and father. My mother spent her last years in a retirement home in Springfield, Missouri, where she remained admirable as always. Although nearly blind, she would count the doors and, locating the right ones, go into the rooms of those who were bedridden, and comfort and cheer them up. I was in my prime then, flying around the country, lecturing here, there, and everywhere. Whenever the talk was remotely near Springfield, I would visit her, but the visits were brief; I was invariably in a hurry. When I would leave the very next day, my mother would hide her disappointment or try to. What would I not give now—I would give anything—if I could enter her room once more and say, "Mother, guess what? This time I will be staying a long time."

My father was already dead by then. In our family we never said, "I love you." His circumlocution to me was, "Huston, we are so proud of you." After a visit, as I'd be leaving, he would point a finger to his cheek, and I would kiss him there. Now I wish I had said it, and said it with all my heart: "Father, I love you, and always have, and always will."

And good-bye to you, dear reader. Writing was to me more than an academic obligation; it was my passion and my refuge. Although we never met in person, you were like a friend, the thought of whom spurred me to my best efforts.

※ ※ ※

A playwright, I can only suppose, fusses over the last line, the one that will bring the curtain down. My last line—how typical of me—is not one but three closing lines as I postpone the curtain, unable to choose which is best.

First close: I echo the British author Elizabeth Pakenham (mother of novelist Antonia Fraser), whose last words were "How interesting, how very interesting it has all been."

Second close: My second last line is actually an observation. The older I get, the more the boundary between me and not-me thins and becomes transparent. I look back upon the paths I have traveled and think, This is me. I look across the table at Kendra, my wife of sixty-five years, and think, This is me. I feel my hip replacement and think, This is me. The childish *oneself versus other* becomes the mature *oneself and other* becomes, finally, *oneself as other.*

And so farewell—but only for now. In some way unforeseen, may we meet again.

Third close: I can choose my favorite closing, after all. It is borrowed from the martyr Saint John Chrysostom, who while being drawn and quartered was said to have exclaimed, "Praise, praise for everything. Thanks, thanks for it all." I savor the words in my mind, roll them on my tongue, and repeat them as my own: *Thanks for everything! Praise for it all!*

APPENDIX

A Universal Grammar of Worldviews *

During the fifteen years that I taught at MIT, my colleague Noam Chomsky made his epochal discovery in linguistics that into the human brain is built a universal grammar that structures every language (English, Chinese, French, German, whatever). In due course I came to see that a universal language of worldviews, of religion, is also embedded in the brain. *Worldviews*—the widest angle of vision, the scheme of things entire—is the accurate word here, but only a minority (those with a philosophical bent) think in these terms. Religion, on the other hand, touches every life in one way or another, so here I will swing back and forth between *worldviews* and *religion,* for (recognized or not) every theology is structured by a worldview.

I lead into my subject by an observation from the *Chandogya Upanishad*:

[A]s by knowing one lump of clay, all things made of clay are known, the difference being only in name and arising from

---

*Originally presented as "A Universal Grammar of World Religions," the fifth annual Master Hsuam Hua Memorial Lecture at the Pacific School of Religion, March 2005.

speech, and the truth being that all are clay; as by knowing one nugget of gold, all things made of gold are known, the difference being only in name and arising from speech, and the truth being that all are gold—exactly so is that knowledge, by knowing which we know all.

This appendix breaks the clay/gold of worldviews into fourteen pieces. They can be thought of as nodules of a geodesic dome over which its encompassing canvas is stretched.

1. Reality is infinite. The Infinite is the one inescapable metaphysical idea, for if you stop with the finitude you face a door with only one side—an absurdity.

2. The Infinite includes the finite or we would be left with infinite-plus-finitude and the Infinite would not be what it claims to be. The image to suggest the Infinite's inclusiveness is a circle, for circles include more space than can any other outline.

3. The contents of finitude are hierarchically ordered. Arthur Lovejoy titled his classic study in the history of philosophy *The Great Chain of Being* and argued that its underlying idea was accepted by most educated people through the world until modernity mistakenly abandoned it in the eighteenth century. The Great Chain of Being is the idea of a universe composed of an infinite number of links ranging in hierarchical order from the meagerest kind of existence through every possible grade up to the boundless Infinite. The ascent may be a smooth continuum, but for practical purposes it helps to divide it into categories—steps on a ladder, so to speak. Aristotle's categorization—mineral, vegetable, animal, and rational—gives us a good start, but it stops too soon, because we rational beings are only halfway up the chain.

4. Causation is from the top down, from the Infinite down through the descending degrees of reality.

5. In descending to the finite, the singularity of the Infinite splays out into multiplicity. The One becomes the many. The parts of the many are virtues, for they retain in lesser degree the signature of the Infinite—of the perfection of the One at the top. The foundational virtue is existence; to be more than figments of the imagination, virtues must exist. The scholastic dictum phrases it as *Esse qua esse bonum est*— "Being as being is good." It is good simply to exist. As for what the virtues other than existence are, India begins with *sat, chit, ananda*—being, consciousness, bliss. The West's ternary is the good, the true, and the beautiful, and these beginnings open out into creativity, compassion, and love until we arrive at Islam's Ninety-Nine Beautiful Names of God. The hundredth name on the Muslim rosary is absent because it is unutterable.

6. Reversing the drift of downward causation, as we look upward from our position on the causal chain we find that these virtues ascend the causal ladder, and as they ascend, their distinctions fade and they begin to merge. This requires that the images of ladder and chain be replaced with a pyramid. Teilhard de Chardin said that everything that rises must *converge,* and this is so. God knows lovingly and loves knowingly, and so on until in the Infinite, differences (which symbolize separation) disappear altogether in the divine simplicity. "Simplicity" here is a technical term; the idea can be likened to a mathematical point that has no extension. To refer to that point, any virtue will serve as long as the word is capitalized, whereupon they all become synonyms. God is

the conventional English for the Infinite, but Good, True, Almighty, One, and so on are all equally appropriate.

7. When the virtues converge at the top of the pyramid, the inbuilt worldview makes its most staggering claim: absolute perfection reigns. In Hegel's dictum, despite the fact that the world is in the worst conceivable turmoil, in the eye of the cyclone all is well. This brings us face-to-face with the problem of evil. Human beings are capable of both great nobility and horrendous evil. Our primary mistake is to put ourselves ahead of others. We cannot get rid of that error, but we can and must work to restrain it. We can reconcile evil with absolute perfection by realizing that it results from misdirected human freedom. God could have made us angels and incapable of misdirecting our freedom, but that slot in the chain of being is already filled. Moreover, it dignifies us to have been endowed with free will, for that ensures than we are not robots.

8. The Great Chain of Being, with its links that increase in worth as they ascend, needs to be qualified by the Hermetic Principle: "As above, so below." Everything that is outside us is also inside us—"the Kingdom of God is within you." We intersect, inhabit, all the echelons of the chain of being. As Sir Thomas Browne recorded in his *Religio Medici,* "Man is a multiple amphibian, disposed to live, not only like other creatures in diverse elements, but in divided and distinguishable worlds."

When we look out, it is natural to visualize the good as up: angels always sing on high and gods live on mountaintops. But when we look inward, the imagery flips and we find that the best things lie deepest within us. The complete picture shows the ineffable, unutterable, apophatic (which is to say unspeakable) Godhead at the top, descending through the personal, describable, cataphatic (speakable) God, then angels, down to the physical universe where we reside. But within us, value inverts and the categories increase in worth. Mind is more important than body, our soul is more important than our mind, and Spirit (which is identical in us all) is more important than soul.

9. Human beings cannot fully know the Infinite. Intimations of it seep into us occasionally, but more than this we cannot manage on our own. If we are to know confidently, the Infinite must take the initiative and show itself to us through revelations. Because there is no commensurability between the finite and the Infinite, truth must be revealed to us. The Infinite discloses itself, as much of itself as our finite minds can comprehend, by building the universal grammars of language and religion into our brains. We did not create those grammars; they were bequeathed to us.

10. When articulated, as in the Bible, the Qur'an, the Upanishads, and the dialogues of Plato, the universal grammars have to be interpreted. Hence the science of exegesis: the critical interpretation of compact worldviews and theologies to unpack their meanings. These interpretations progress through four stages of ascending importance: the literal, the ethical, the allegorical, and the anagogic. First, the literal: what does the text explicitly assert?—that the Buddha was enlightened under the Bodhi tree and so on. Next, the ethical: what does the text explicitly tell us that we should do? Third, the allegorical meaning: illustrative stories and so on. Finally, and most important, the anagogic: what is the text's capacity to inspire us?

11. All these factors were taken for granted until the rise of twentieth-century fundamentalism with its obsession with

the literal. Fundamentalism has generated so much confusion that it justifies a little excursus to indicate what its mistake is. Science points the way to the mistake.

Science has shown us that there are three great domains of size: the microworld of quantum mechanics, where distances are measured in picometers; the macroworld that we live in, where distances are measured in feet, yards, and miles; and the megaworld, where the distances are measured in light-years. Now, scientists know that there is no way to talk consistently about domains that flank ours—those of the microworld and the megaworld—while using ordinary language. You would run into contradictions at every turn, like those that cartographers run into when they try to depict the globe on the two-dimensional pages of a geography book. You can't do it accurately. The Infinite—God, or whatever you want to call the Ultimate—is at least as different from our everyday world as are quantum mechanics and relativity theory, for the sufficient reason that the Infinite includes both of those. The scientists recognize that they cannot describe their domains consistently in everyday language. Still, they can understand those domains by using science's technical language, which is mathematics. The same goes for worldviews. The only way we can access the upper levels of reality that climax in the Infinite is by using the technical language of worldviews and religion: symbolism. Symbolism is the science of understanding the relations between the multiple levels of reality. It includes poetry, music, dance, art—and prose when it deals inspiringly with the Ultimate.

12. There are two distinct and complementary ways of knowing: the rational and the intuitive. The life and career of Blaise Pascal throw the two into exceptionally sharp

relief. When he exclaimed, "The heart has reasons the mind knows not of," the mind he was thinking of was his scientific mind, through which he achieved fame for his theory of probability in mathematics and his work on hydrodynamics in physics. And *heart* was his word for the organ through which there burst the epiphany that turned his concern from science to religion: "Fire! God of Abraham . . . Isaac . . . Jacob. Not the philosophers and the learned. Tears of joy . . . my God, let me not be separated from Thee forever." But that he never intended to dismiss philosophy and learning is amply evidenced by his eighteen closely reasoned *Lettres Provenciales* in which he examined the fundamental problems of human existence. It is also evidenced by the fact that he titled the entries into his notebook *Pensées,* in which he spells out his conviction that the true function of reason is to attain the truth or supreme good.

All religions carefully spell out the distinction between reason and intuition. In the West, intellect (*intellectus, gnosis, sapentia*) is not reason (*ratio*); in Sanskrit, *buddhi* is not *manes;* in Islam, *ma'rifah,* situated in the heart, is not *aql,* which is situated in the brain. In Hinduism, the knowledge that effects union with God is not discursive; it has the immediacy of direct vision, or sight.

13. Walnuts have shells that house kernels, and religions likewise have outsides and insides. The outer, exoteric forms house the interior, esoteric cores. The difference in the way people relate to the two comes down to how adept they are with abstraction. Esoterics are comfortable with abstractions, whereas exoterics require that ideas be concrete and representational if they are to be clear. It follows that exoterics like to think of the Infinite in personal terms, whereas esoterics,

while subscribing to the idea of the Infinite-clothed-in-human-attributes, are at the same time aware of the danger that such clothing can easily turn into anthropomorphism, into making God too human. So it needs to be supplemented by esotericism. We need for God to be like us so we can connect with him. But we also need God to be unlike us, because we cannot worship ourselves.

14. Finally, what we know is ringed about with darkness. It is a numinous darkness that lures us, for we know that God sees it as light, and at times we sense a kind of twilight zone around its edges. But to cognition the darkness remains. We are born in ignorance, we live in ignorance, and we die in ignorance. In relation to the Infinite we stand as less than a simple protein in a single cell on a human finger. Though it is alive, that protein cannot know the cell in which it lives. How then can it conceive of the skin, the knuckle, or the finger's articulating joints, the intricacies of the ligaments, nerves, and muscles, the electrobiochemical process of that finger of which it is a negligible part? And even if it could contain all that understanding, it could never conceive of the whole hand of which it is a part, which can find expression in the fingering of a guitar, the fist clenched in anger, the delicate touch needed for surgical repair of the heart. It is only a simple protein, an amino-acid building block.

So much less are we in this mass of the universe and beyond it, the Infinite. Once again: we are born in mystery, we live in mystery, and we die in mystery.

ACKNOWLEDGMENTS

HUSTON SMITH'S ACKNOWLEDGMENTS

It remains my pleasant duty to thank the following friends:

Kendra, my wife, suggested the title for the book and has corrected many memories that the book contains. She also served ably as the book's first-round editor.

Eric Brandt, Senior Editor at HarperOne, helped me to believe in this book and has kept the book on course as it progressed.

Jeffery Paine stands in a separate category, for, unlike the above, he had no vested interest in me but was willing to interrupt *his* publishing schedule to be the coauthor of *my* book. In consequence my gratitude to him is unbounded, not only for what he made of this book, but for the fact that in the process of working on it with him I gained a friend.

JEFFERY PAINE'S ACKNOWLEDGMENTS

My share of this book is dedicated to

Kendra and Huston
with much friendship and such affection

and to Molly Friedrich, jewel among agents,

and to Eric Brandt, gem among editors,

and to wonderful Linda and Jerry and Margot.

CREDITS

PHOTO CREDITS

All photos are from the author's personal collection except for the following:

Central Methodist College Photographs courtesy of Central Methodist University

Henry Weiman, Photo courtesy of Jim Nugent/the Unitarian Universalist Historical Society.

Gerald Heard, Permission by The Barrie Family Trust

Max Beckmann, Erich Lessing / Art Resource, NY

Werner Heisenberg, Keystone/Getty Images

Eleanor Roosevelt, ©SV-Bilderdienst / The Image Works

Tiananmen Square, Photo by Chris Niedenthal/Time Life Pictures/Getty Images

David Bohm, AP Photo

Robert Oppenheimer, Photo by Gaby'Pix Inc./Time Life Pictures/Getty Images

Martin Luther King, Jr., Photo by Michael Ochs Archives/Getty Images

T.S. Eliot, Photo by John Gay/Hulton Archive/Getty Images

Thomas Merton, Photo by Sibylle Akers, used by permission of the Merton Center Archives

Krishnamurti, ©Mary Evans Picture Library / The Image Works

Huston Smith with Keisaku, ©Heng Sure

Tibetan Chanting, ©Boston Globe

Three Steps One Bow ©Heng Sure

Photograph of Frithjof Schuon courtesy of World Wisdom

Masai Tribesman, Photo by Charles Ommanney/Getty Images

Oren Lyons, Photo by Charley Gallay/Getty Images

Eileen Garrett, ©Mary Evans Picture Library / The Image Works

Death Valley, GABRIEL BOUYS/AFP/Getty Images

Aldous Huxley, Photo by Murray Garrett/Getty Images

Timothy Leary, ©Topham/The Image Works

INDEX

Page numbers of photographs appear in italics.